New Ways in Teaching Writing

Ronald V. White, Editor

New Ways in TESOL Series

Innovative Classroom Techniques

Jack C. Richards, Series Editor

Teachers of English to Speakers of Other Languages, Inc.

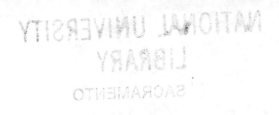

Typeset in Garamond Book and Tiffany Demi
by Automated Graphic Systems, White Plains, Maryland, USA
and printed by
Pantagraph Printing, Bloomington, Illinois USA

Teachers of English to Speakers of Other Languages, Inc.
1600 Cameron Street, Suite 300
Alexandria, Virginia 22314 USA
Tel 703-836-0774 • Fax 703-836-7864

Director of Communications and Marketing: Helen Kornblum
Senior Editor: Marilyn Kupetz
Editorial Assistants: Cheryl Donnelly and Lance Savage
Cover Design and Spot Art: Ann Kammerer
Part Title Illustrations: David Connell

ISBN 0-939791-57-9
Library of Congress Catalogue No. 94-061425

Table of Contents

Introduction

In her review of the teaching of writing, Ann Raimes (1991) showed how theories and uses of writing have developed over the past quarter century. Whatever the theory, and whatever the methodology employed, writing has always had an important place in language teaching. Until the development of cheap sound recording equipment, writing was virtually the only way of obtaining evidence of a learner's performance, either as a record of what they could do, or as material for evaluation, as in written tests and examinations.

Indeed, the permanence of writing has always given it a high status, to the extent that ability to write in a foreign language has commonly been taken as the only acceptable evidence of proficiency. The great rise in interest in spoken communication, characteristic of the past 20 years, has challenged the status of writing. The development of oral testing combined with cheap and effective means of recording has reduced reliance on writing as evidence of proficiency. Ability to speak a foreign language has become a more highly rated skill than being able to write in it. Even so, writing in a foreign language such as English still remains an important requirement for many learners, especially given the role of English in international communication and commerce. As a result, writing in English has now become an end in itself, and not just a means of displaying linguistic achievement.

Likewise, writing, while retaining a significant learning role in language pedagogy, is now seen to have an important function in empowering learners in the world outside the classroom. Undoubtedly one of the most notable influences on the teaching of writing has been the set of principles and procedures associated with the process approach (see Krapels, 1990; Silva, 1990; Susser, 1994; Zamel, 1987)—an approach that has stimulated some controversy in the pages of *TESOL Quarterly* (Hamp-Lyons, 1986; Horowitz, 1986; Leibman-Kleine, 1986).

Writing can be viewed as involving a number of thinking processes which are drawn upon in varied and complex ways as an individual composes, transcribes, evaluates, and revises (Arndt, 1987; Raimes, 1985). Writers, it is clear, have highly varied ways of composing, and any writing task involves a highly creative use of composing processes. Although there are differences between composing in a first and second language, there are many common underlying processes (Krapels, 1990; Silva, 1993). Typically, a writer has to

- produce relevant ideas
- evaluate these ideas in relation to purpose, topic, and audience
- consider the knowledge, attitudes and tastes of the intended reader
- make decisions about the amount of information shared with the reader, the kind of information that has to be made explicit and the need for indirectness
- take account of the separation in time and place between writer and reader
- conform to conventions of style and format in the social group concerned
- conform to grammatical and other language conventions
- organize and structure ideas, content and purposes into a coherent whole
- write a draft
- revise and improve the draft
- produce a final version to be published in some way.

In addition to these, a writer may have to work to a deadline. It is scarcely surprising, then, that writing is a challenge. Being blocked as a writer often means not being able to produce relevant ideas, and it is here that a number of techniques can be used to overcome the block. Such techniques, sometimes called *heuristics* (Hughey, Wormuth, Harfield, & Jacobs, 1983), include brainstorming, mapping, outlining and fastwriting. What they have in common is a focus on content and meaning. And because brainstorming encourages an uninhibited approach to idea generating, a writer has freedom to give priority to producing ideas before involving questions of judgment and evaluation. Writing is not just an ideas free for all, however. It is also a social process involving a reader who is to be engaged in some way by the writer. Such engagement doesn't have to be profound—it may only be a fleeting capturing of attention, long enough to communicate a simple message.

Nonetheless, it is important for the writer to win the reader's attention, interest, and involvement. Achieving this will require giving some thought to where the reader is coming from; in other words, what does the reader already know about the subject, what attitudes does the reader have about it, what does she want or need to know, what will it take to influence or affect her? Even on a simple, everyday level, a writer would have to consider the answers to such questions when, for instance, writing a note to arrange a meeting. "See you at the office at 3" may make sense to the writer, but the message will only make achieve its purpose—a successful rendezvous—if by "the office," writer and reader mean the same place.

Although writing is traditionally regarded as a solitary process, with the isolated writer communicating with an individual reader, learning to write can usefully benefit from being a social process. There are a number of reasons for this: First, apprentice writers need to have rapid response from readers if they are to develop social awareness as a writer. Second, feedback is an important part of skill development—readers reacting to a draft will provide this. Third, collaboration can be a significant way of enhancing effective learning (Hedgcock & Lefkowitz, 1992). We learn from each other, and we learn to contribute to each other's learning and development through collaboration. Finally, locating writing in a social context places it right in the center of an active, interactive classroom methodology.

Learning to write cannot be separated from reading (Eisterhold, 1990). Reading can provide content, ideas, guidelines and models. Identifying useful information, comprehending a writer's purpose and viewpoint, selecting key ideas, following the organization and development of ideas—these are all reading skills relevant to writing. Writers must be readers, and they may need to evaluate, interpret and summarize what they read so as to provide input to their own writing. Thus, summarizing and paraphrasing become important writing skills based on reading. Synthesizing material and ideas from different sources will draw on such summaries and notes. Drafting—or committing to print—is the process of converting thoughts to tangible form.

Once a draft has been produced, it can be evaluated as a way of developing or improving it. This can be done by the writer, or better still, by other readers. In the teaching setting, the other reader is usually the teacher. Placing the burden of reading drafts on the teacher ignores an important resource already present in the classroom: other learners. The peer group can and should be involved in evaluating each other's drafts, learning from and contributing to each other.

In moving from one draft to another, writers begin to shape the text to conform to organizational and format conventions. Ideas are not simply assembled in random order. Lines of text are not simply scattered across the page in a disorderly fashion. Writers find that they have to organize their moves in a way which is logical to a reader. There must be coherence. Likewise, the display of text upon the page requires organizing into visual units which reflect the organizational structure while also helping the reader to make their way through the text. For many types of writing, there are very explicit organizational and format conventions which writers are expected—or even required—to follow. Learning and applying these conventions is part of the induction into the writing community.

All of the considerations just outlined are incorporated in this book. Contributors have provided an extensive range of activities that develop different composing skills, attend to the social processes of reading and writing, involve the peer group in evaluating and responding to drafts, focus on different types and formats of writing, and stimulate these activities through diverse techniques and methods.

The book is organized in four parts, each of which deals with a different aspect of writing.

Part I Writing processes: from generating ideas to completing stories, using critical thinking, evaluating and revising

Part II Academic writing: from paragraph to essay by way of e-mail and sentence joining

Part III Expressive writing: creative and personal writing, including poetry and prose

Part IV Personal and business correspondence: writing in the "real" world.

Contributors have used a variety of techniques, some familiar and some new, with some original and creative variations on familiar procedures.

Some also exploit technology, such as using cassette recorders to provide feedback or exploring the possibilities of e-mail for responding to other writers in a continuing dialogue.

A wide range of different text types is also covered, including different types of correspondence—notes, post cards, personal letters, business letters, office memos, letters to the press, letters of complaint. Familiar types of writing are covered—descriptive, narrative, discursive, argumentative and comparative prose—as well as biography, reports, fables and tales, diaries, posters, and poetry. There is even some work on writing in exams and under timed conditions.

This book is not intended to provide a definitive and exhaustive array of techniques and procedures. Rather, it is a resource to be drawn upon as a way of supplementing existing techniques. Experienced teachers will find useful variations to enliven and extend their existing repertoire, while less experienced ones will discover a range of procedures that they can try out and adapt as part of the process of developing their own skills as a writing teacher.

References

Arndt, V. (1987). Six writers in search of texts: A protocol-based study of L1 and L2 writing. *ELT Journal, 41,* 257–267.

Eisterhold, J. C. (1990). Reading-writing connections: Toward a description for second language learners. In B. Kroll (Ed.), *Second language writing: Research insights for the classroom* (pp. 88–101). Cambridge: Cambridge University Press.

Hamp-Lyons, L. (1986). No new lamps for old yet, please. *TESOL Quarterly, 20,* 790–794.

Horowitz, D. (1986). Process not product: Less than meets the eye. *TESOL Quarterly, 20,* 141–144.

Hughey, J. B., Wormuth, D. R., Harfield, V. F., & Jacobs, H. L. (1983). *Teaching ESL composition: Principles and techniques.* Rowley, MA: Newbury House.

Krapels, A. R. (1990). An overview of second language writing process research. In B. Kroll (Ed.), *Second language writing: Research insights for the classroom* (pp. 37-56). Cambridge: Cambridge University Press.

Leibman-Kleine, J. (1986). In defence of teaching process in ESL composition. *TESOL Quarterly, 20,* 783-788.

Raimes, A. (1985). What unskilled ESL students do as they write: A classroom study of composing. *TESOL Quarterly, 19,* 259-258.

Raimes, A. (1991). Out of the woods: Emerging traditions in the teaching of writing. *TESOL Quarterly, 25,* 407-430.

Silva, T. (1990). Second language composition instruction: Development, issues and directions in ESL. In B. Kroll (Ed.), *Second language writing: Research insights for the classroom* (pp. 11-23). Cambridge: Cambridge University Press.

Silva, T. (1993). Toward an understanding of the distinct nature of L2 writing: The ESL research and its implications. *TESOL Quarterly, 27,* 657-677.

Susser, B. (1994). Process approaches in ESL/EFL writing instruction. *Journal of Second Language Writing, 3,* 31-47.

Zamel, V. (1987). Recent research on writing pedagogy. *TESOL Quarterly, 21,* 687-715.

Users' Guide to Activities

Cohesion

Part II: Academic Writing

Paraphrasing and Summarizing

Synthesizing

Revision

Examination Writing

Portfolios

Part III: Expressive Writing

Stories and Narratives

Fables and Proverbs

Biography

Poetry and Verse

Journals

Descriptive Writing

Part IV: Personal and Business Correspondence

Personal Correspondence

Business Writing

Part I: Writing Processes

Editor's Note

One of the most notable features of current approaches to teaching writing is the emphasis on fluency rather than accuracy—although accuracy still remains an important concern. Undoubtedly, inhibitions about starting to write will limit fluency, so writing teachers have given a lot of thought to ways of reducing constraints and developing confidence, and a number of techniques for doing so are found in this section.

One approach is to use prompts, such as visuals and real objects, to stimulate ideas. Another is to use headings and questions so that the writer has a framework for support. A third approach is to adapt such idea-generating techniques as brainstorming, in which students are encouraged to produce ideas in a nonjudgmental manner. Finally, variations on free or fast writing, in which students write as much as they can as quickly as they can while suspending judgment on quality or accuracy can also be used to overcome the fear of starting. Clearly, writing without inhibition, while usefully overcoming reluctance or difficulty, will probably result in a somewhat incoherent draft, and this is where learning to organize and shape ideas and text becomes important.

Learners can analyze examples of good writing, or they can practice putting scrambled sentences and paragraphs into order. Such activities help to develop an awareness of the significance of logical ordering and of ways of signalling meaning relationships to a reader.

Form communicates meaning, so attention to expression remains important. Learning to use participial and adjectival clauses, for instance, is a way of developing precision and sophistication in writing. The drafting and development of writing involves processes at different levels. Writing can be regarded as a problem-solving process in which writers employ a range of cognitive and linguistic skills to enable them to identify a purpose, to produce and shape ideas, and to refine expression.

◆ Pre- and Freewriting On the Other Hand . . .

Levels
Intermediate +

Aims
Devote energy to
writing

Class Time
40–50 minutes

Resources
Pen and paper

Some students perceive themselves as being handicapped by their language ability. Energy that might better be used to compose is spent fretting over difficulties in stringing sentences together in a meaningful way. This activity—having to write the words of each speaker in a two-way dialogue using different hands—introduces a different handicap in order to refocus the students' attention on the text and away from themselves. It can be done at any time during the term and supplements the composition work students normally do.

Procedure

1. Ask the students to divide a piece of paper in two lengthwise.
2. Tell them that they will be writing a dialogue between two speakers. Speaker A's part of the conversation will be written with one hand on the left side of the paper; Speaker B's will be written with the other hand on the right side.
3. Tell them that they will probably find it difficult to use the hand they don't normally use. However, because scientists claim that the left and right hands are controlled by opposite sides of the brain, we can expect to see a very different personality for each hand.
4. Remind them not to try to think about what to say before beginning. Rather, they should start writing and let what one character says lead naturally into the other character's response—just like a real conversation. They should write for approximately 15-20 minutes or until they have filled one to two sheets.

5. While the students are writing, you should be doing the same. If done on the board, this will serve to demonstrate that you are having as much difficulty as they controlling your nonwriting hand.

6. When sufficient time has passed, go around the room and have people share their compositions. Students will probably be surprised at how different the personalities of the respective hands are. Whether or not it has anything to do with the left and right sides of the brain, you will probably note that the students have been able to get a lot written in a short time. In addition, many will probably report that they spent less time thinking about their language ability than they normally do.

Contributor

Paul Arenson is Teacher-in-Charge, Intermediate Level, at the International Education Center, in Tokyo, Japan.

It All Started With an Apple

Levels
High intermediate +

Aims
Think creatively,
exploring multiple uses
of an image in writing
Develop strategies for
fluency, speed, free
flow of ideas

Class Time
45 minutes

Resources
One whole, fresh, shiny
apple/student

Prewriting or invention strategies help students access their existing knowledge about a topic before they begin to plan an essay. This activity is based on the technique of freewriting, or looping, in which writers set to paper everything that comes into their heads, no matter how loosely connected, for a set period of time. One objective is to free the writer from the constraints of structure and to encourage a period of free association of ideas. A second objective is to help students discover the many possible directions in which a topic may be developed.

Procedure

1. Bring to class a bag full of apples and give one to each student, along with a paper towel or napkin. Give the students these directions:

   For today's activity, you need to have a pen or pencil and some paper. I have given you an apple—and that is your writing topic for the next 15 minutes. When I tell you to begin, you will start writing about your apple. You may write anything that comes into your head, and you do not need to worry about spelling or grammar or style. The only rule is that you may not stop writing, not even to think. If you cannot remember a word in English, just write the word in your language and keep writing. If your mind goes blank, write the words "I can't think of anything to write" over and over until at last you think of something else to write. Remember: Your pen must keep moving across the paper for the entire 15 minutes; do not stop writing.

2. When you are certain that everyone understands the instructions, give the signal to begin writing. During this activity, if students ask what they should do with their apples, I try to be noncommittal by shrugging my shoulders and not responding.

3. While the students write, you may elect to write about the apple also. Writing with one's students is a well-respected way of demonstrating the value of the task and of discovering one's own response as a writer to the work. Often, however, instead of writing about the apple, I stand or sit to one side of the room with a pad of paper and a pen, and I take ethnographic notes about the students' actions as they write, noting where they put the apples, who eats the apples and who does not, what their individual writing and apple-munching habits are, and so on. I try to write something about each student in the class, and to find patterns in their behavior.

4. When 15 minutes are up, ask the students to reread silently what they've written and then to write a single sentence that summarizes or otherwise says something important about what's on their paper. Then tell them to continue writing for another 10 minutes. (This step can be omitted if time is short.)

5. At the end of this 10 minutes, stop the writers again and tell them to put their pens down.

6. At this point, I reveal my role as an ethnographer, and I tell them about my observations. I describe their different writing styles: Some sit very still, moving only the fingers of their writing hand; some shift position frequently and run their fingers through their hair or jiggle their feet or engage in some similar manifestation of nervous energy; some eat their apples with gusto; others hold the apples delicately in their laps or abandon them on an adjacent desk. I do this only after having established an environment of trust and good will in the classroom; it's important to me not to embarrass or alienate students. My goal is to call attention to the variety of valid ways in which people think and work and write; later we may continue this thought by surveying the students' homework habits too. Another benefit of this part of the activity is that it allows students to "decompress" a bit from the intensity of their concentration on writing.

7. After everyone has laughed and relaxed, I ask for volunteers to read all or part of what they've written. Usually, in spite of some early hesitation, everyone ultimately agrees to share his or her apple-writing. The outcome here is unpredictable: I have laughed, cried, applauded, and sat in stunned silence, listening to the endless variety of the

students' connections. Invariably, the entire class is deeply impressed by the awesome diversity of the responses and by the unexpected emotionality of the writing. We celebrate the creativity of the work, and we brainstorm about ways to develop these writings into full essays. I leave it up to the students to decide individually if they want to work further on this topic; some always do.

Contributor

Alice Gertzman is a graduate student in the Department of Linguistics and Modern English Language at Lancaster University in the United Kingdom.

Charting Stereotypes in Literature

Levels
Intermediate +

Aims
Analyze a piece of
literature and discuss
stereotypes found in it
Put information in table
form as part of drafting

Class Time
1 hour

Resources
None

This activity encourages students to recognize stereotypes in literature and to evaluate those stereotypes in terms of their validity and fairness. The activity promotes critical thinking via reading, discussion, and writing. The charts students produce are a starting point for many different types of writing.

Procedure

1. Divide students into groups of four.
2. Invite each student to write the title of a fairy tale or fable that each has read.
3. Ask each group to choose one of the titles and summarize the story orally to make sure they remember the story.
4. Have each group make a chart with three column headings: Character, Category(s), and Characteristics (see Appendix). The story's main characters are listed in the chart's first column. The category(s) to which the character belongs, for example, their sex, race, social class, are listed in the second column. The third column is for a description of the characteristics of the character.
5. Encourage everyone to actively participate, by assigning one or more characters for whom they complete Columns 2 and 3. Group discussion follows. The absence of certain categories of characters can also be noted.
6. Have groups discuss whether the characteristics of the representatives of each category actually exist in real life. Are the characterizations stereotyped or fair?
7. The chart and the discussion can result in various activities including:

   • writing reviews of the story in terms of its stereotypes and giving it a grade (e.g., A–F, the least stereotyped to the most stereotyped)

- writing argumentative essays based on whether students agree/disagree with the way the story presented the characters
- rewriting the narrative to avoid unfair stereotypes, for example, changing the characteristics of characters, changing the plot
- writing accounts of students' own experiences with stereotypes

Appendix: Chart Analyzing *Cinderella*

Character	Category(s)	Characteristics
Cinderella	Female Poor person, but originally rich	Beautiful, passive, kind, helpful, hardworking, interested in clothes
The stepmother and stepsisters	Female Rich people	Ugly, jealous, mean, lazy, interested in clothes
The prince	Male Rich person	Handsome, active, generous, interested in beauty, source of money
Fairy godmother	Female Elder person	Caring, giving the young help and advice
	People of color	Absent from story

Contributors

George Jacobs is a language specialist at the SEAMEO Regional Language Centre, in Singapore. Maygala Devi Ramadass teaches English and Chemistry at the Technical School of Ipoh, Malaysia.

Tell and Transform

Levels
Intermediate +

Aims
Improve the content
and quality of writing

Class Time
2–5 periods

Preparation Time
20 minutes

*K*nowledge telling means that you just write down everything you can think of just as it comes into your mind. This is a common first approach to writing and is possibly the only approach available to children and to other beginning writers. *Knowledge transforming* means that basic knowledge is developed, shaped and organized so that the student's own structure is imposed on the material (Bereiter & Scardamalia, 1987).

Procedure

1. Give students a topic and ask them to write all that they can about it.
2. Ask students to examine what they have written sentence by sentence and to try to develop their ideas about each aspect of the content. Point out that their first draft is a telling-all-you-know exercise and that they should now think of ways to develop these basic ideas.
3. Introduce them to the concepts of *knowledge telling* and *knowledge transforming* and help them understand the differences.
4. Encourage students to re-examine what they have written and to try to identify common themes which can be linked together. At this stage they should also re-examine their material to find out if they have moved on conceptually since they last thought about these ideas. This is the point at which new ideas may be created and alternative ways of looking at the content may emerge.

Encourage them also to value this part of the task and to view it as a means of reviewing not only what they think they know but also the opinions they hold. It is important to reconsider the arguments one is accustomed to putting forward in order to find out if they are still acceptable or if, in the light of new information, they now need to be reassessed and updated.

5. Several drafts may be necessary before the move—from telling all that is known in an unstructured way to an acceptable draft that transforms the initial content into an quality product—is accomplished.
6. Once the content reads acceptably for meaning, a final editing exercise should be undertaken. Editing will of course have been an integral part of the whole drafting process, but a major effort should now be undertaken to ensure that the final product is as accurate as possible.

Encourage students to take this part of the exercise very seriously and to be aware that careless editing will undermine their whole effort. Topics should be kept very simple until students get used to the technique.

References and Further Reading

Bereiter, C. G., & Scardamalia, M. (1987). *The psychology of written communication*. Hillsdale, NJ: Lawrence Erlbaum.

Contributor

Carol MacLennan has taught in multicultural schools in New Zealand, in universities in Shanghai and Macau, and is currently involved in teacher education in Hong Kong.

Finding Wild Mind

Levels
Beginning +

Aims
Relax and enjoy writing
by focusing on ideas
rather than mechanics

Class Time
15 minutes

Resources
Pen, paper, topic

Natalie Goldberg (1990) writes about Zen and the art of writing in *Wild Mind: Living the Writer's Life*. She states,

> That big sky is wild mind. I'm going to climb up to that sky straight over our heads and put one dot on it with a Magic Marker. See that dot? That dot is what Zen calls *monkey mind* or what western psychology calls *part of conscious mind*. We give all our attention to that one dot. So when it says we can't write, that we're no good, are failures, fools for even picking up a pen, we listen to it. (p. 32)

We need to give ESL students techniques to help them relax, get their thoughts to flow, and write with confidence. There is plenty of time later to edit.

Procedure

1. Give students the theoretical underpinnings and goals of this type of writing activity as outlined above.
2. Tell students that they will write for 10 minutes without stopping and that their hands will probably hurt because this is a long time to write without stopping.
3. Present the following "rules" for writing practice (Goldberg, 1990) and thoroughly review these rules with students. (If possible, play beautiful background music while the students write.)

   a. Keep your hand moving. Don't stop. The purpose of this is to keep the editor and the creator from becoming mixed up. "If you keep your creator hand moving, the editor hand can't catch up with it and lock it."
   b. Lose control. "Say what you want to say. Don't worry if it's correct, polite, appropriate. Just let it rip."

c. Be specific. "Not car, but Cadillac. Not fruit, but apple. Not bird, but wren."

d. Don't think. Find wild mind.

e. Don't worry about punctuation, spelling, grammar.

f. You are free to write the worst junk in the world.

g. Go for the jugular. "If something scary comes up, go for it. That's where the energy is." Have students mine the gems of the writing practice exercise to find something that they can work with and develop. Now is when students should edit, revise and rewrite so as to produce a "finished" piece. (pp. 2-4)

References and Further Reading

Goldberg, N. (1990). *Wild mind: Living the writer's life*. Bantam Books.
Root, C. (1991, Winter). From monkey mind to wild mind. *MATSOL Newsletter*.

Contributor

Christine B. Root is a teaching fellow in ESL at Harvard University, Boston, Massachusetts, in the United States.

Solving Problems While Prewriting

Levels
Low intermediate +

Aims
Inform and persuade

Class Time
10–40 minutes

Resources
Paper, guidelines for problem-solving heuristic

ESL student learning to write have to deal with a new environment in which determining a reader's background, attitudes, and receptivity to the writing can pose significant problems. The method described below includes a combination of prewriting, freewriting, and problem-solving techniques.

Procedure

1. Give students the background information and necessary input documents (e.g., incoming letters, reports, raw data) to describe a situation requiring some action in the form of a memo, letter, or report (e.g., a letter from a local school board member requesting a list of titles, prices, and discounts for books the firm sells and also requesting help in convincing the other school board members that the library holdings need to be expanded).
2. For the introductory session, lead the group in working through the following problem-solving heuristic; after the first exercise, have the students work individually or in groups. Assign groups of about five so that, if possible, there is a cross-section of subject majors and abilities.
3. Write out responses to each of the following steps, using freewriting and brainstorming:

   - Facts—Use brainstorming, mapping, outlining methods to identify the facts in the situation; include obvious facts as well as assumptions.
   - Objective—Identify the objective of the message, including details on the desired response of the reader(s).
   - Reader—Visualize the reader, including age, educational level, cultural/work/home background, present orientation to the situation, and values (those relating to the specific situation and those general

values that probably affect the reader's whole mode of operation and framework of behavior).

- Medium—Identify a medium (e.g., letter, report, personal visit).
- Appeals—Determine what motivation to use in appealing to the reader's need and convincing the reader (e.g., nostalgia, efficiency, family love, status, profit).
- Topic—Define the topic in terms of the appeals, rather that in terms of the objective. For example, if the appeals are *economy, status,* and *good educational services,* the topic for a proposal to convince a school board to increase the library holdings would be: How allocating money for library books will save money, allow students to broaden their horizons to be able to better cope with a complex world, and improve the education and the reputation of the school district.
- Organizational Plan—Select an effective organizational method and strategy for accomplishing the objective (e.g., indirect and persuasive)
- Outline—Sketch out a rough summary of what needs to be included in the beginning (commend them on working so hard to improve educational opportunities), middle (describe the importance of education, of seeking and sharing knowledge, and the efficiency of books), and end (offer to help by making available for selection a wide range of titles and good services so that they can achieve their objective of providing excellent education for the students in the community).

4. To involve students even further in active problem solving, use graphic methods such as the scattergram and box outlines or card outlines to help the student draw connections between the facts.

5. Evaluate the plans appropriately (teacher, self, peer, or group), but address only ideas and organization; students should not be required to use complete sentences or even to check spelling. (If assigning points to the task, a full-credit participation grade would be appropriate.)

6. Group interaction skills can be taught during the problem-solving process so students develop cooperative learning skills, serve as peer

teacher, endure peer pressure to perform, and develop a camaraderie that improves classroom climate and promotes student receptivity). In addition, students (e.g., business students) can use these exercises to practice leadership and participation skills necessary for success in their future careers.

7. If possible, have students write a rough draft based on the comments, and ask them to use a writing center, tutor, or grammar/style-checking computer program in polishing the draft before submitting the full document.

8. The problem-solving plan can also provide the students with an evaluation technique that they can use on their own writing or on a peer's writing. Ask the students to work backwards from the final product, from evaluating the writing to determining whether the result (the composition) is consistent with the topic, addresses the reader's perspective, and will probably accomplish the purpose.

Contributor

Janet Winter is Associate Professor in the Department of Management at Central Missouri State University, in the United States.

◆ Beginning-Level Developmental Work
The Rainbow Game

Levels
Beginning

Aims
Describe various objects
Express an opinion

Class Time
20–25 minutes

Resources
Worksheet for each
student (see Appendix)

This activity reviews vocabulary items and enables students to express original ideas and opinions using the vocabulary.

Procedure

1. Ask the students to suggest four colors that they like and write those four colors as the headings of four of the five columns on their worksheets. The fifth column is left blank.
2. Dictate a list of 20 familiar nouns. Have students write each word in one or more columns, according to what they decide is the most appropriate color.
3. As one student read his list aloud, classmates guess which color was intended.
4. Have students label the fifth (blank) column with a favorite color and then write four to six vocabulary items for that color.
5. Students take turns reading their color lists as their classmates guess which color they intended.

Caveats and Options

This activity can be used as a vocabulary review at any level. More advanced students can use their lists as starting points for short compositions.

**Appendix:
The Rainbow
Game
Worksheet**

The Rainbow Game

Contributor

Leslie Cohen teaches at the Kibbutz Ein Hashofet, Israel.

The Sun, the Moon, and the Stars

Levels
Beginning +

Aims
Compare and contrast
in simple sentences

Class Time
15 minutes

Resources
Chalkboard and chalk
(for teacher)
Pencil and paper (for
students)

This task challenges students to think and allows them to express their opinions, even with limited vocabulary. It encourages creative thinking and puts value on individual differences. While allowing for the expression of a wide range of ideas and opinions, it also facilitates accuracy.

Procedure

1. Draw three simple pictures on the chalkboard: a sun, a moon, and several stars.
2. Ask: "Which two are alike and why? What makes the third different?"
3. Explain that there are no right or wrong answers and that it is interesting to hear the variety of ideas that students have.
4. Write model sentences on the chalkboard:

   The _____ is/are like the _____
   because .... The _____ is/are different because ....

5. Give students 5 minutes to write their opinions.
6. Share aloud.

Caveats and Options

This activity can be done at any level. It can be used with other cues, pictorial or verbal. It can be repeated in the same class a number of times, using different cues.

Contributor

Leslie Cohen teaches at the Kibbutz Ein Hashofet, Israel.

Scrambled Sentences in Envelopes

Levels
High beginning–
intermediate

Aims
Practice basic sentence
patterns in a task-based
activity
Practice using reference
clues to construct
sentences without using
pencil and paper
Sharpen proofreading
skills

Class Time
20 minutes

Preparation Time
15 minutes

Resources
One envelope and 26
pieces of paper/group

The advantage of these activities is that students are not required to write out sentences, nor are teachers burdened with papers to mark and return. The feedback is instantaneous. In sum, the activities offer an enjoyable way to practice basic sentence structure and simple composition points, and the students enjoy the competition.

Procedure

1. Write several simple sentences on a sheet of paper. Leave ample space between the sentences and cut them into several pieces. (Possible places to cut are marked with an asterisk.)

   Yesterday the weather was nice, so * I went * to the park * with my friends.
   He works * from Tuesday * to Saturday, * so he can't play golf * on Saturday.
   There are 6 people * in my family.
   Susan gave * her teacher * a letter from her mother.
   The soccer players * are very happy * because they won the match.
   Of all the countries * in South America * Brazil is * the largest and * Chile is * the longest.
   A taxi driver * doesn't accept * credit cards for payment.

2. Explain what a scrambled sentence is. If necessary, put an example on the board.
3. Divide class into pairs or groups. Have students clear one area of the table or desk so that everyone in the pair/group can help in constructing the sentences.
4. Give each pair/group an envelope. Have students empty the contents and count the number of sentence pieces. Using the above sample sentences, there should be 26 pieces.

5. Set a time limit of 10 minutes. Have the students work as quickly as possible to construct the sentences. Walk around the room and give hints to students who are having some difficulties. Obvious clues should be the capital letters and punctuation. However, other points to focus on are references clues (*my, her*) semantic clues (e.g., geographical terms, days of the week), and grammatical clues (e.g., singular subjects take singular verbs).

Caveats and Options

Instead of having everyone work on the same set of sentences, prepare five to seven envelopes. Each envelope should have three or four sentences cut up into pieces. On the outside of each envelope, write a number on the envelope and the number of pieces inside (e.g., Envelope Number 4; 13 pieces). You will need more envelopes than pairs/groups. For example, if you have five groups, you will need about eight envelopes for this activity. Write the name of the pairs/groups on the board. Have each pair/group choose one envelope and begin working at the same time. When students have finished, they should raise their hands and you should then check their work. If all sentences are correct, all the pieces should be put back in the envelope. Write that envelope number by the students' name on the board (because they have successfully completed that envelope). The students should then choose one of the remaining envelopes. This task can continue for a set time limit or until one pair/group has done all of the envelopes.

This alternative has a faster pace than the original exercise and is often more entertaining for the students. However, the advantage of the original exercise is that you can review all of the constructed sentences with all of the students very easily. This is often of great importance when teaching low-level classes.

Acknowledgment

A former teaching colleague, Beth Powell, showed me this idea.

Contributor

Keith S. Folse is the author of several ESL texts published by the University of Michigan Press.

It's All in the Name

Levels
Beginning +

Aims
Practice listening to
writing, face-to-face
communication, spelling
Participate in a
nonthreatening, student-
centered writing class

Class Time
20–30 minutes

Resources
Chalkboard

Students often go through a whole course without properly learning to address each other in the way that they wish to be addressed. The first class is the time to set a personal and communicative agenda by getting students to focus on language that belongs to them—their names. You can help set the tone for the class by having the students lead you toward the correct pronunciation of their names. This activity, as a first exercise in a writing class, lends itself to face-to-face communication and has a high probability of communicative success. The accomplishment, though seemingly simple and pedestrian, is real and useful, not least because it recognizes the importance of a person's name and the value of honoring students as individuals.

Procedure

1. Ask all of the students to come to the board and write their first and last names.
2. Pronounce each name and ask that person to give you feedback on your pronunciation. Keep going until each person gives some sort of positive feedback on your pronunciation.
3. Ask students to try to pronounce any names of their classmates that they find to be different for them. Practically, this means names of students from dissimilar cultures; for example, a Mexican student trying to pronounce a Vietnamese name. Again have the student whose name it is give feedback.
4. Tell students that they must move around the classroom and ask 10 different students for their first and last names. Of the 10 names, half must be from cultures and countries other than their own. For example, a Japanese student would need to have at least 5 non-Japanese names in a list of 10 names.

23

5. Students must dictate their names to one another by using the English alphabet.
6. The exercise is over when students have written down their 10 names.

Caveats and Options

1. After each student has collected 10 names, ask some students to read from their list to the class. Have the class take dictation while the student reading the name introduces the person. Invite students to speculate about the person being named. Invite that person to reply. For example, a student might speculate that another student named Kim Il Hwon comes from the Republic of Korea. That student would then say something like, "I think you are from Korea." Kim Il Hwon might reply, "Yes, I am," or "No, my name is Korean, but I am from Japan."
2. Especially at lower levels, the teacher might want to write the alphabet on the board to refer to during the exercise.
3. Again, especially at lower levels, the teacher might want to provide a list of pertinent questions and requests for students to use in the exercise. Some of these might be:

   a. How do you spell your first name?
   b. How do you spell your last (family) name?
   c. Please repeat that.
   d. Say that again, please.
   e. Was that *i* /ai/ or *e* /i:/?

Contributor

Lou Spaventa teaches in the summer MAT program, School for International Training, Vermont, in the United States. Marilynn Spaventa teaches at Santa Barbara City College, California, in the United States.

From Sentence to Story

Levels
Low intermediate

Aims
Convey meaningful
ideas using a variety of
complex sentences

Class Time
1 hour for each of the
two target structures

Resources
Grammar book with
explanation of target
structure with examples
Text with numerous
examples of the target
structure
Handouts

This activity enables students to write meaningful, complex sentences using some variety of target structures. Students move from a controlled stimulus of sentence pairs to self-generated sentences.

Procedure

1. Go through the textbook explanation of the target structure together with the students.
2. Using a portion of a narrative reading containing examples of the target structure, have students work in pairs to underline all the examples of the target structure.
3. Go over the examples the students have found and help students with any problems or questions.
4. Put some sentence pairs on the board and have the class help you combine them using the target structure for one of the sentences.
5. Give students a handout with several sentence pairs to combine. This is best if composed from information in a reading the class has already done. Three pairs is a good sample. (See Appendix, Worksheet 1.)
6. Have the students work in pairs to combine the sentence pairs.
7. Have some students put their new sentences on the board and go over the sentences together with the class.
8. Finally, give students an untitled beginning of a story with 6–10 sentence pairs to combine. (See Appendix, Worksheets 2 and 3.)
9. Have students combine the sentence pairs using the target structure.
10. Instruct students to finish the story using three to five complex sentences of their own with the target structure.

Appendix: Student Worksheets

Student Worksheet No. 1

Instructions: The following pairs of sentences contain information from the reading in your text, "No-Fat Nation," by James Fallows. Combine these sentences to make one sentence using a participial phrase for one of the sentences.

1. Americans worry about being fat.
   Americans have a huge exercise industry.
2. The Japanese eat a lot of vegetables and little fat to stay healthy.
   They have very few exercise clubs.
3. Tokyo is a very crowded city.
   Tokyo doesn't have enough space for sports.

Student Worksheet No. 2

Instructions: Combine the following series of sentence pairs using a participial phrase for one of the sentences. When you finish this, you will have the beginning of a story. Think of an ending for the story. Then, using a participial phrase for each sentence, write two or three sentences to complete the story. Give the story a title.

Note: Read the entire story out loud. It should sound like a poem. Why?

Title: _____

1. The wind rocked the boat.
   It blew water over the deck.
2. The clouds moved quickly across the sky.
   The clouds were dark and ominous.
3. The sailor brought in the sails.
   He pulled the ropes vigorously.
4. He stashed the remaining food below deck.
   He felt very alone and worried.
5. Lightning flashed brightly across the sky.
   It was both beautiful and horrible.
6. He thought of his sweetheart at home.
   He wished he were with her now.

Now write two or three sentences of you own to complete this story. Each sentence should contain a participial phrase.

Student Worksheet No. 3

Instructions: Combine the following pairs of sentences to create complex sentences. You will need to make one sentence into a dependent clause or participial phrase. There are several possibilities for each pair. (Try to use a variety of clauses and phrases.) You will need to write an ending for the story using your own complex sentences. When you are done, choose a title for your story.

Title: _____

1. Thirteen-year-old Brian Crain fastened his seatbelt.
   He looked intently at the plane's control panel directly in front of him.
2. The 72-year-old pilot was kind and patient.
   He carefully explained to Brian how to work the controls.
3. The pilot started the engine of the "Celsa."
   The "Celsa" was a small two-person plane.
4. The "Celsa" rose quickly over the field and headed from Vancouver toward the Canadian wilderness.
   The Canadian wilderness stretched for hundreds of miles in all directions.

Finish the story: Using six complex sentences of your own and a variety of dependent clauses (adjective, adverbial) or phrases (participial), write your own ending of the story.

Story ending:

5.
6.
7.
8.
9.
10.

Students Answers for Worksheet No. 3

1. Fastening his seatbelt, 13-year-old Brian Crain looked intently at the plane's control panel directly in front of him.

   As 13-year-old Brian Crain fastened his seatbelt, he looked intently at the plane's control panel directly in front of him.

   After he had fastened his seatbelt, 13-year-old Brian Crain looked intently at the plane's control panel directly in front of him.

2. The 72-year-old pilot, who was kind and patient, carefully explained to Brian how to work the controls.

   Being kind and patient, the 72-year-old pilot carefully explained to Brian how to work the controls.

   Because the 72-year-old pilot was kind and patient, he carefully explained to Brian how to work the controls.

3. The pilot started the engine of the "Celsa," which was a small two-person plane.

4. The "Celsa" rose quickly over the field and headed from Vancouver toward the Canadian wilderness, which stretched for hundreds of miles in all directions.

   The "Celsa" rose quickly over the field and headed from Vancouver toward the Canadian wilderness that stretched for hundreds of miles in all directions.

Contributor

Mary Ullrich teaches at the Intensive American Language Center, Washington State University, in the United States.

Guided Sentence Expansion

Levels
Intermediate

Aims
Describe

Class Time
20–40 minutes

Resources
Picture of one or more people in a striking or unusual setting, or with a pet

Using this technique, students experiment with and practice expanding sentences with vivid, clear vocabulary and develop skills in using particular grammatical patterns. Because students are only dealing with one sentence at a time, the task is easily controlled, and because they can add whatever they want, the students have the freedom to write distinctive sentences. The amount of writing is small enough that group or class peer response or correction is not overwhelming.

Procedure

1. Using a picture, ask students for a very simple sentence. Write this on the board, leaving a lot of space between words.
2. Ask students to suggest additions to the sentence, using one or more of the following: adjective; adverb; a relative clause with *who*, *that*, *which*; a subordinate clause with *because*, *when*, *if*; participial adjectives (phrases); a comparison (with *like*, *as if*, *as . . . as . . .*). You can also elicit additions by asking *wh*-questions, e.g., "Where is this lake?" "How old are they?" "What is her name?" "Whose suitcase is that?" "Why are they going there?"
3. Write suggestions on the board, asking students where the additions should go, and working together on correct grammar and vocabulary.
4. Bring out one or more new pictures. Have students work individually or in pairs. You can start everyone off with the same simple sentence or have them make one. Give students two or more specifications to add, or questions to answer, depending on their level and how much time you have to spend on this exercise.
5. Ask students to write their sentences on the board. You can check students' sentences before they put them on the board, or you and the students can correct them together from the board. If students

had a choice of pictures, sentences for the same picture should be put up together for comparison.

6. Make sure to comment admiringly on one thing in each sentence, for example, a particularly descriptive adjective, an evocative *if*-clause or comparison. Then elicit any necessary corrections (or explain why a suggested correction is not necessary).

Appendix: Sample Original and Expanded Sentences

Original: *A woman is sitting on a bench.*
Expanded (uncorrected):

An old woman, who wear the glasses, is sitting on a swing bench with a small yellow puppy infront of the country style cafe, waiting for a bus.

In front of a cafe shop, a poor lady with glasses sitting on a red swing bench next to a small cute dog is looking aside, like waiting for somebody to show up.

A middle-aged woman from South Carolina is sitting with her brown puppy on a red swing in-front of an old style cafe, looking with empty eyes in the distance, expecting for the afternoon train to arrive.

Expecting someone, an aged woman with black glasses is sitting at a red rusty swing outside an old cafe with a little white dog stretching beside her.

In the outside porch of a cafe, an old woman is sitting on a red swing with a skinny little dog next to her, looking at nowhere, waiting for death to come and take her away.

A insane woman, who has a wild dog with her, is sitting on a swing in front of a cafeteria and waiting for her husband who has been lost for years.

Contributor

Lise Winer teaches in the Department of Linguistics, Southern Illinois University, Carbondale, in the United States.

◆ Generating Ideas
Silent Brainstorming

Level
Intermediate +

Aims
Generate ideas, using a
cooperative, written
approach in class

Class Time
15–20 minutes

Resources
Large file cards (or
sheets of paper)

This activity helps student writers generate ideas for topics that they have chosen but not thought much about. It invokes cooperative learning and peer input analogous to brainstorming: Its freedom, creativity, and lack of inhibition are of great value in prewriting. By doing this activity—silent (written) brainstorming—every student writer gets some input on his or her topic from several others, and every student contributes in an intensive way. The writer of the essay receives many written comments and questions, some of which may turn out to be valuable stimuli, at the start of the prewriting phase.

Procedure

1. Distribute a file card to each student. Instruct the students not to put their names on the cards. Tell each student to write her or his new topic at the top of the card, followed by one brief statement about any aspect of the topic that might be developed in the essay.
2. Have the students hand the cards to you. Shuffle them and distribute them randomly around the class. Inform the class that a student who gets his own card must treat it as if it were a card from another student, to maintain anonymity as far as possible.
3. Tell the students that they will have 1 minute in which to read what is on the card and write a comment or a wh-question about it immediately below the statement written by the originator of the card. (You can write this instruction on the board, as well as speaking it.) Emphasize that the comment or question must in some way be related to the topic, but that it does not have to be too closely related so that there is scope for free and creative thought on the part of the person reading the card. Also tell the students that you will not read or grade these cards, which will be returned directly to their originators. This

ensures that the students feel they are giving input to a peer, not to the instructor, and they feel less inhibited. Remind them to write legibly.

4. After about 1 minute (you can tell when most students have finished writing), instruct the students to pass the card to the person on his or her right.

5. Repeat Step 3 again and again. Announce that each successive reader may also write questions or comments about the questions or comments of preceding readers. Occasionally remind them to let their imaginations go so that their peers will have fresh and interesting ideas to work on. Gradually increase the time permitted for reading the cards and writing on them to about 2 minutes, to allow for the increasing number of comments and questions on each card.

6. When you judge that there are enough questions and comments on the cards, collect them and distribute them to their originators by calling out the topic, which students can use to identify their own cards. Ten questions or comments usually provide enough food for thought for the authors.

7. Instruct the student writers to reflect carefully on the input from their peers and to use their questions and comments as springboards for further idea development. Make it clear that it is entirely up to them, as authors, to make use of or ignore the peer input when drafting their essays.

Caveats and Options

1. Use sheets of paper instead of large file cards.
2. Have students write their names on the cards if you feel there is no need to preserve anonymity.
3. Instead of stopping the activity after a specific number of comments or questions, stop only when all students have written on each card.

Contributor

Lionel Menasche teaches in the English Language Institute at the University of Pittsburgh, Pennsylvania, in the United States.

FRIEDs: A Development Device

Levels
Intermediate +

Aims
Develop ideas in the prewriting, drafting, and revising stages of the writing process

Class Time
10–20 minutes

Resources
Chalkboard, overhead (OHP), or prepared handouts

Students are frequently frustrated when confronted with academic writing assignments. Not only must they contend with a variety of language demands, (e.g., vocabulary, syntax, audience, tone, orthography, discourse patterns), but they are all too often instructed to develop their ideas without further guidance as to what this entails. As students learn written English, they learn that writing less affords fewer opportunities to make mistakes. Thus, they begin to seek safe routes to completion of an assignment, routes they might not take in their L1s when they could allow their thoughts deeper and more fully developed consideration. English FRIEDs help students develop their initial and incomplete considerations.

Procedure

1. Write the acronym

   F
   R
   I
   E
   D

   vertically on the board or OHP. While writing, explain that this is a technique to develop ideas when students find themselves saying, "I don't know what else to say, and you're telling me to develop this." Continue to explain that this heuristic will help them over this common rough spot and may ease them into much wider consideration than a little list might otherwise seem to offer.

2. Explain the word that each letter stands for, beginning with the *F*.

   - ***F** stands for Facts*. These are pieces of information known to be true or proven. Frequently facts include numbers, such as dates,

34

statistics or other figures, such as amounts of money. But they can include any proven statement as well, such as *The earth is round*, *The sun rises*, or *This teacher is a tough grader*.

- *R stands for Reasons.* A brief warning should be issued here because reasons may also create a grammatical trap. Even though we use them every day, for example, *Because we think this way*, they may also cause fragments if left incomplete.
- *I stands for Incidents.* An incident is described as something that happened to you or someone you know. A major advantage of incidents is that they contain many rich details that the writers already know and can consequently use more readily in the written work. Usually of a narrative quality, incidents tend to be longer than the previous acronym items and can release or ease students away from the fear of more words equals more mistakes.
- *E stands for Examples.* Examples of examples may seem at first repetitious and redundant but because there are several types of examples, it is helpful to explain. Examples always follow words such as: *such as, for example, for instance*, and sometimes *like*, to create additional specific development of a general idea: *He likes Italian food, for example, spaghetti and lasagna*. Examples can also demonstrate a specific idea without the use of alerting terms, just as the example of key words above functions as an example.
- *D stands for Details.* Most commonly details may be defined as adjectives and adverbs that add the spice and color to an otherwise unfocused vision.

3. At this point, students usually begin to sort: Which are details and which are examples? It is thus necessary now to explain how the acronym works as a generating device: The FRIEDs create ways to grow but are not meant to function as labels. Each of the FRIEDs is meant to create a jumping-off point but does not exist in a separate cell, that is each one is not a discrete entity. Instead as a group they tend to overlap; for example, an incident can function as an example and be filled with facts, reasons and details. Therefore, if a student tries to deconstruct an essay to see how the FRIEDs are used, he may not be able to tell where one element starts and the other leaves

off. But that is acceptable since they are meant to generate specific development of student ideas.

4. Make students aware that they may pick and choose from the list, that not all will work (nor should they) for a given paper and certain audiences and purposes, but that they present choices in the form of a mnemonic, an easily accessible device.

Caveats and Options

1. The FRIEDs are certainly not meant to be an exhaustive way of looking at development but do offer a distinct advantage: ESL writing students, often for the first time, discover specificity as an obtainable goal. A barrier to more complex writing is removed when they have tangible tools.

2. Alert students to the following: Because academic writing all too often requires writing under time limitations, the FRIEDs function as a mnemonic device, an immediate check against panic because the items in this list are easily seized upon when students are under duress.

Appendix: Worksheet, Handout, Visuals

(Only necessary if no chalkboard is available.)
Sample student writing before FRIEDs:

> I saw movie I like very much. It was about girl who did not have many friend. She met boy and become friend of him. They stay good friend. They did many thing together. However he die. Everyone were so sad. Her father could not help her.

An early assignment after presentation of the FRIEDs (and peer/teacher feedback):

> Last Saturday, my cousin, Thuy, and I went to see a movie called *My Girl* at the Edwards Theater in Alhambra. The main character was a ten-year-old girl named Sam, who had no friends until she met Davey, a new boy in town. They shared a warm friendship and together they went fishing, swimming, and bicycling. They also shared their feelings about death.

Suddenly Davey died. No one could comfort Sam, even though her father, the mortician, and his girlfriend, the cosmetologist, tried. At last she discovered that her life had to continue although she missed her friend very much.

I enjoyed the movie because it reminded me that children also have deep feelings and they should not be ignored. I will try to be kinder to my younger sisters now. We can learn much from the movies.

Contributor

Karen A. Russikoff teaches in the College of Arts, California State University, Pomona, in the United States.

The Most Important Advice

Levels
High intermediate +

Aims
Develop invention
strategies

Class Time
45–50 minutes

Resources
Handout of invention
questions

This activity, stimulating the students to examine the deeper cultural meanings of the advice about life they have received, helps them learn how to ask pertinent questions, as an invention strategy, in order to explore a composition topic in depth.

Procedure

1. Ask the students to recall the most important advice about life they have received from their parents or an older relative or friend. (An example either from yourself or somebody else would be helpful.) Have them write it down in brief notes.
2. Ask the students to write quickly and informally to respond to the following questions. Explain to them that they are writing to facilitate their thinking, so they needn't worry about grammar, spelling, punctuation, and neatness. They should, rather, concentrate on capturing their thoughts in words on paper.
3. Write these questions on the chalkboard or supply them on a handout:

   - Have you heard the same advice before? Do other parents give their children the same advice? Have you encountered similar advice given by characters to their children in a novel or play? Have you read about similar advice in newspaper articles, history, biography, or any other books?
   - Why do your parents, relative, or friend think it is important to give you this advice? What special circumstances prompted them to give this advice?
   - Why do you think the advice is important? Can you recall any religious or philosophical teachings that make you believe it is important?

- Are boys and girls given the same advice? If not, what are the differences? Why do they receive different advice?
- If you were a parent, would you give the same advice to your children? Why, or why not? Do you think that 100 years from now, people in your country will still give the same advice to their children? Why, or why not?
- What are the positive consequences if you follow the advice? What will be the negative consequences if you don't follow the advice? Why do you think there will be such consequences?

4. Organize the students into groups of four. Make sure that each group is composed, to the greatest extent possible, of students of different nationalities.
5. Ask the students to talk about the advice they have written down and their thoughts in response to the questions about it.
6. Have them write quickly and informally again—this time to respond to "What are the similarities and differences between the most important advice you have received and that the other students have received? Why are they similar or different?"
7. By now, the students will have generated a substantial number of ideas about the advice and at the same time gained a better understanding of the cultural context of the advice. They're ready, in the next step, to discover a focal point for an expository essay on the most important advice they've received.

Contributor

George Q. Xu teaches in the Department of English, Clarion University, in the United States.

Creative Stimulus—Creative Response

Levels
Any

Aims
Develop creative and
critical thinking skills

Class Time
30–40 minutes

Resources
Notebook (or
notepaper) that can be
divided into four
columns
Stimulus (e.g., an object
participants do not
recognize; a quotation;
a section of text)

This activity gets students to observe objects/texts carefully and critically, to draw upon their vocabulary to respond to a stimulus, and to think creatively/critically about the stimulus. In addition to allowing students to use language, to share perceptions, and to come to new understandings, the activity also reinforces the concepts of objectivity versus subjectivity. The activity is a starting point for a series of exercises designed to teach students how to use a dialectical notebook, a tool that can be used to enhance their reading, writing, and thinking.

Procedure

1. Have students bring to class unknown objects, that is, things that their classmates may not be able to identify. (Note: In a class made up of students from different cultures, participants should bring objects that look like something else from another culture. For example, in the United States, a wire egg holder—of the type used to dip Easter eggs in dye—can be intellectually challenging, as students from other cultures may have no idea what such an object could be used for.)
2. Divide students into groups. (Groups of four work best, although triads are also successful.)
3. In their notebooks have students make creases in two pages facing each other, so that they end up with four columns, two on each page. Have them label the columns in this order: Column 1 = *Observations*; Column 2 = *Questions/Need to Know*; Column 3 = *Peer Response*; Column 4 = *Further Reflection*. (You may want to write sample responses—words, phrases—so students understand that they don't need to write essays.)

4. Assign each group an object with which they are not familiar. (If students have brought a number of mysterious objects, choose the best ones and assign one object to each group.)

5. Have students work in Column 1 (Observations). Ask them to pass their object around the group. As they do so, have them write observations about/descriptions of their object in that column. Remind them that they do not need to have the object in hand in order to describe it. Warn students not to make any subjective, interpretive statements ("It's a rubber toy"). The first column is for objective description only. If there are any questions regarding vocabulary for the descriptions, you should supply that vocabulary. Have students pass the object around the group a couple of times; ask them to make closer and closer observations each time to note what they may have missed on the first go-rounds. At this stage, encourage students just to write their responses rather than to discuss their observations with each other.

   As teacher/facilitator, you may want to reinforce the concepts of *objectivity* and *subjectivity* while the students are writing in the first column. Make the observation that things are not always what they seem and that, in fact, we, as human beings, are prone to inferences/conclusions that are hasty generalizations.

6. When students have completed their note-taking, have each member of the group read his observations to the group; have the groups discuss their descriptions—what they have observed objectively about the object, what vocabulary is necessary to describe/characterize it. (If there is no one word or phrase that accurately describes the object, have students use figurative language: *It looks like my car key.*)

7. Next, have the students work in Column 2 (Questions/Need to Know). In this column, have students make comments and write questions about the objects that may help them to come to an understanding of what the object is (e.g., *Looks like something used in the kitchen. Could it be used to cut vegetables?*) At this stage of the process, students should engage in subjective interpretation of the object.

8. When the students look as though they have written enough questions, have them discuss their questions and possible answers. The more questions the better. In addition, gentle disagreement is helpful here. If, for example, one student insists something must be used in the kitchen as a cutting tool, another may disagree, observing that the object is not sharp enough to be used for cutting. Careful observation and critical thinking are necessary at this stage of the process.

   Walk around the class and monitor the discussions. If students appear frustrated by the exercise, intervene and alleviate their frustration by doing something such as asking a question that directs their attention to a particular aspect of the object.

9. After some initial discussion, have students move to Column 3 (Peer Response). Ask students to make notes in this column on the discussions they have had and to incorporate ideas they have gained from their peers. Have students attempt to come to some conclusions about the object, based on their discussions.

10. Ask each group to identify the object—that is, its name (if they know it) and its use. (You may ask more questions if you think they will help students identify the object.) Each group should come up with a number of plausible identifications (possible uses for the object); however, if they do not come to the correct conclusion, have them do Column 4 (Further Reflection) as homework. By this point, they may be frustrated—craving an answer—or they may have had their curiosity piqued.

10. To achieve closure to the activity, have students read from their Further Reflections during the next class session. Discuss the comments a bit more; identify the object for the students.

Caveats and Options

1. If students are interested in the exercise, you may repeat the procedure, assigning a second object to each group. Once students have learned to use this notebook format, you can use the format for different purposes. The unknown object exercise described above is good to start with, as it uses a concrete object and can be used as a self-contained exercise.

2. It can also be used in conjunction with discussions on hasty generalizations and about how our perceptions are shaped by our cultural backgrounds. By extension, insights gained from the exercise can be used in group discussions on the more abstract topic of cultural misunderstanding—of how visitors to foreign cultures may be misled by perceptions of what appears to be so, when, in fact, the reality of the situation may be quite different.

3. Later, instead of objects, you may substitute quotations, sections of text from the students' readings, notes students have taken from their readings, vocabulary prompts (e.g., freedom of choice), to stimulate writing, thinking, and discussion. Although you may need to modify the labels of the columns, the basic format will remain intact, and you will ask students to respond to stimuli; to ask questions about them; to come to tentative hypotheses/answers; to share their questions/perceptions with their peers; and then to do further reflection on the ideas generated.

Contributor

Norman J. Yoshida teaches in the Institute for the Study of American Language and Culture, Lewis and Clark College, in the United States.

◆ Organizing Paragraphs
Paragraph Consequences

Levels
Intermediate +

Aims
Draft and revise a
paragraph

Class Time
1 1/2–2 hours

Resources
Topic sentence on a
subject likely to spark
students' interest
Overhead projector
(OHP) and
transparencies

This activity makes students aware of the importance and nature of coherence in paragraphs. It could follow work on lexical and grammatical cohesion in texts and semantic markers and could lead on to the writing of longer texts such as essays. The collective nature of the activity promotes students' uninhibited evaluation of their own writing.

Procedure

1. Explain the purpose of the activity and the procedure to students.
2. Divide the students into small groups. Each student should have pen and paper. You may decide to participate in one or two of the groups yourself.
3. Write the topic sentence on the board and ask the students to copy it onto their paper. If desired, a different topic sentence can be given to each group for greater variety at the final revision stage.
4. Ask each student to write the second sentence of the paragraph and to pass their paper to their neighbor. Each student then writes the third sentence of the paragraph and passes the paper on again. Thus, each paragraph grows as the papers go round the group.
5. When each paragraph consists of four or five sentences, ask the student to write a closing sentence and pass on the paper for the last time. The students should then read their paragraph and check that it ends appropriately; if they feel that it does not, they can add a final sentence.
6. There are now several possibilities for revising and providing feedback. If there is sufficient time, ask students to edit all the paragraphs (individually or in groups) and write them on the transparencies or large sheets of paper so they can be studied by the whole class. If less time is available, each group can select the best and the worst

of its paragraphs, edit them and write them on transparencies. If time is very short, editing can be left until the next step.

7. Finally, display the paragraphs for the whole class to see. Ask students to comment on the strengths and weaknesses of each and to suggest improvements.

Appendix: Sample Sentence

Here is an example of an opening sentence that has produced some interesting paragraphs:

Finding suitable accommodation is becomingly increasingly difficult for students in (name of city).

Contributor

Don Dunmore teaches in the English Language Unit at the University of Leeds, in the United Kingdom.

Paragraph Unity

Levels
Low intermediate +

Aims
Become aware of
cohesive devices and
sequence in paragraphs

Class Time
10–20 minutes

Resources
Authentic paragraphs
retyped as individual
sentences and cut into
strips
Photocopies of the
original paragraphs with
sources acknowledged

Contributor

This activity helps students to discover for themselves how cohesive devices contribute to the readability of English paragraphs.

Procedure

1. Arrange the students in groups of three to six people.
2. Give each group a set of strip sentences from one paragraph. Their task is to arrange them into their original order.
3. When a group has achieved some (not necessarily complete) success, give them another paragraph to work on. It is not necessary for students to discover the exact original order of the sentences, but the order they propose should be reasonable.
4. After repeating the process a few times, show students the original paragraphs, and discuss the clues that they used to discover the hidden order of the sentences. Also point out other clues they may have missed.

Ron Grove is Associate Professor in the Department of Area Studies, Mejiro University, Iwatsuki, Japan.

Patterns

Levels
Intermediate +

Aims
Work with an
organizational
framework for an essay
and paragraph

Class Time
1 hour

Resources
Student worksheet (see
Appendix)

This activity is based on a chapter in a particular reading textbook (see reference), but could easily be adapted to other readings.

Procedure

1. Copy and distribute worksheets.
2. Divide the class into small groups.
3. Ask students to list ideas that could be effectively supported by the organizational patterns listed on the worksheet.
4. When group work is completed, write student examples on the chalkboard for class discussion.

Caveats and Options

1. Have students examine previously written student essays for organizational patterns.
2. Ask students to match topic sentences from previously written essays with organizational patterns that could effectively support the idea.
3. Have students write topic sentences that could be effectively supported by each organizational pattern.
4. Have students write essays or paragraphs based upon a specific pattern.

References and Further Reading

Adams, T. W. (1989). *Inside textbooks: What students need to know.* New York: Addison-Wesley.

Appendix: Student Worksheet

Organizing Your Ideas Effectively

1. Chronological order or reverse chronological order
   Examples: _____
   _____

2. Order of importance (most to least or least to most)
   Examples: _____
   _____

3. Known to unknown
   Examples: _____
   _____

4. Cause and effect
   Examples: _____
   _____

5. General to specific statements/specific to general
   Examples: _____
   _____

6. Problem and solution
   Examples: _____
   _____

7. Whole to parts
   Examples: _____
   _____

8. Concept to description
   Examples: _____
   _____

9. Similarities and differences
   Examples: _____
   _____

Contributor

Michele Kilgore is an ESL instructor at Georgia State University. She has an MS in Applied Linguistics and is working on her doctorate.

◆ Cohesion
Putting Sentences Together

Levels
Low intermediate +

Aims
Expound an idea or to argue for or against a position

Class Time
30–40 minutes

Preparation Time
30 minutes

Resources
Any piece of writing that uses connectives, for example newspaper articles, editorials, letters to the editor, magazine articles, student writing

Students who write sentences well still have difficulty joining sentences logically and cohesively. It is, therefore, important that students practice presenting their ideas or arguments logically. It is also essential to help students link their ideas and improve cohesiveness in their writing. This activity helps students develop logical thinking by arranging jumbled sentences in a logical order, showing the relationships between ideas by using appropriate connectives.

Procedure

1. From a newspaper or magazine article, select a paragraph that contains at least 10 sentences and several connectives.
2. Delete all connectives.
3. On a sheet of paper, type each sentence of the paragraph on a separate line.
4. Make enough copies for student groups of four.
5. For each copy, cut, and jumble up all the sentences.
6. Distribute these sentences to each group.
7. Ask members of each group to arrange these sentences in a logical sequence and then supply connectives where appropriate.
8. Ask each group to write up the paragraph.
9. Have the class compare and discuss their work.

Caveats and Options

1. Write the connectives on the chalkboard for low-level students and ask them to choose the most appropriate ones in linking the sentences. Advanced students should be allowed to use connectives of their own choice.
2. Student writing that shows effective use of connectives may be chosen as the text in Step 1. The class discussion suggested in Step 9 may

prove motivating and encouraging as students are shown what they themselves are capable of achieving.

3. Student writing that shows inappropriate use or lack of connectives may be chosen as the text in Step 1. This will raise students' awareness of the weaknesses in their writing and provides a chance for self-monitoring.

Appendix: Student Writing Samples

These sentences are taken from a letter to the editor in a local newspaper. All the connectives have been removed. Each sentence is typed on a separate line. Each group of students will receive all the sentences which have been cut out and jumbled up. Then they are asked to arrange the sentences in a logical manner and supply appropriate connectives.

The number of young smokers has increased recently.
They enjoy smoking.
It helps them relax and they enjoy the taste.
They think smoking is a fashion.
They think if they don't smoke, they will not be accepted by their peers.
Smoking is bad for their health.
There is a need to help them kick the habit.
The government should put more emphasis on health education.
Youngsters should be told the risks of smoking to discourage them from starting and encourage them to quit.
Such a measure is more effective than using posters.

Student Work

The following shows the writing completed by two groups of students. All the connectives have been chosen by the students and italicized by me. The two different versions suggest the flexibility of this activity. More advanced students should be given the freedom to choose their own connectives and arrange the sentences in any order as long as it is logical and demonstrates coherence. The final class discussion on the choice of different connectives and arrangements may provide good opportunities for clarifying concepts and increasing awareness of linguistic requirements in writing.

Sample 1

The number of young smokers has increased recently *because* they think smoking is a fashion. They believe that if they don't smoke, they will not be accepted by their peers. *Besides,* they enjoy smoking *because* it helps them relax and they enjoy the taste. *However,* smoking is bad for their health, *so* there is a need to help them kick the habit. The Government should put more emphasis on health education *as* such a measure is more effective than using posters only. Youngsters should be told the risks of smoking to discourage them from starting and encourage them to quit.

Sample 2

The number of young smokers has increased recently. They enjoy smoking *because* it helps them to relax and they enjoy the taste. *Besides,* they think smoking is a fashion *as* they believe that if they don't smoke, they will not be accepted by their peers. *However,* smoking is bad for their health. *So* there is a need to help them kick the habit. *Furthermore,* the Government should put more emphasis on health education. Youngsters should be told the risks of smoking to discourage them from starting and encourage them to quit. Such a measure is more effective than using posters.

Contributor

Judy Ho teaches in the English Department of the City University of Hong Kong.

Strip Story and More

Levels
Low intermediate +

Aims
Organize and recognize logical order in expository writing Identify and use topic sentences and concluding sentences for transitions between paragraphs to provide cohesion

Class Time
50–60 minutes for the strip story
50–60 minutes for the additional activities

Resources
Expository papers at students' reading level
One envelope/paragraph of the story
One overhead transparency/paragraph
Transparency pens
Overhead projector (OHP)

The writings of many ESL and EFL students, perhaps because of cultural differences, seem disorganized to the U.S. reader. This activity helps students recognize how a writer uses word repetition, expansion of ideas, and connective adverbs to provide cohesion within paragraphs and transitions between paragraphs. The exercises are ordered so that students first learn to identify logical order and later get guided and independent practice.

Procedure

1. Find an expository essay from the students' reading text or from a magazine. Make sure the paper is at your students' reading level. Cut the expository paper into sentence strips. Put strips into envelopes, one envelope per paragraph.
2. Divide the class into the same number of groups as you have paragraph envelopes. Give each person in each group one or two sentences from their paragraph envelope.
3. Ask each group to put their sentences into logical order to complete a paragraph.
4. Once they have agreed upon the best sentence order, ask students to write their paragraph onto a transparency.
5. After all the groups have completed their transparencies, put one of the transparencies on the OHP for the whole class to see. All of the students read and discuss the order of the sentences and make suggestions if they have any. Point out repetition of words, ideas and connectives that work as transitions Ask students to identify topic sentences and concluding sentences. Continue until all of the paragraphs have been discussed by the whole class.
6. Ask the class to put the paragraphs in logical order. Discuss reasons for the order chosen.

Caveats and Options

1. In subsequent sessions, pair students and ask them to unscramble more sentences and paragraphs from other expository papers.
2. Have students identify topic and concluding sentences in other expository writing.
3. Omit topic and/or concluding sentences from paragraphs and ask students to write their own topic and concluding sentences. This can be done in pairs or individually.
4. Give the students topic sentences only and ask them to write a paragraph that might follow such a topic sentence.
5. Ask students to write their own expository papers, reminding them to use topic and concluding sentences that provide smooth transitions between paragraphs.

Contributor

M. R. Sayavedra teaches in the School of Education's TESOL program at Oregon State University, in the United States.

Connecting Up

Aims
See the role of
repetition, pronoun
reference, and
transitional devices in
paragraph coherence
Practice pronoun/
antecedent agreement
and appropriate
transitions

Resources
Copies for every student
of a paragraph in which
blank spaces replace all
pronouns, repetitions of
key words, and
transitional words or
phrases
Chalkboard
Colored chalk

Procedure

1. Divide students into groups of three or four and provide each of them with a copy of the paragraph.
2. Ask students, working in their groups, to fill in the blanks. Allow them 10–15 minutes to complete the task.
3. Moving around the groups, have students report on and discuss the rationale behind their choices for filling in the blank spaces. Cross-check with the other groups and encourage further discussion whenever a divergence of opinion arises.
4. Fill in each blank in the paragraph on the chalkboard with the students' choice before moving on to the next. If a consensus is not reached, record all choices.
5. When all blanks are filled, show students the original paragraph. Ask them to discuss any discrepancies between it and theirs and the significance of the connecting lines.
6. Identify and discuss any problem areas the exercise has revealed. Discrepancies in pronoun reference, for example, provide an opportunity to review pronoun/antecedent agreement in general.

Appendix: Sample Handout

The words in bold are those deleted from the copy handed out to the students.

Camel racing in the Arabian Peninsula is an example of a tradition that has evolved into both a social and a scientific institution. Wealthy sheikhs provide financial support and prize money that assures bedouin owners of **racing** camels, as well as **their** trainers and jockeys, of secure futures without **their** having to forsake **their** nomadic

54

way of life. **At the same time,** owner sheikhs, competing among **themselves**, have transformed the sport. Today it is an **institution** as organized and as scientifically sophisticated as horse **racing** is elsewhere. **Camel** clinics, fitted out with the latest available technology, have been established. Veterinarians are employed to provide care and treatment for the **camels**, both at the **clinics** and in the bedouin camps. **They also** conduct **sophisticated** research: on embryo transplants, on the cross-breeding of different **camel** strains, and on the development of training techniques based on studies of the **camel's** physiology. The **sport** succeeds, **therefore**, in balancing past and present, both by supporting the **nomadic** way of life and by promoting **scientific** research.

Contributor

Margaret Shabka is Director of the English Language Center at the University of Maryland, Baltimore County, in the United States.

Part II: Academic Writing

Editor's Note

For many students and teachers, academic writing has high priority because writing is such a significant activity within college-level education. Students who are unable to write academic essays will be marginalized within the academy. Consequently, developing academic writing skills becomes a means of empowering students, although the extent of the writing teacher's responsibility for inducting students into the discourse community of their subject discipline remains a debating point (see Braine, 1988; Johns, 1988; Spack, 1988).

Within academic writing, the link between reading and writing is highly important. Reading provides content as well as models. Students need training in summarizing and paraphrasing so that they can abstract ideas from sources and present them within the context of their own writing. Students can also usefully use examples of academic writing as a guide to conventions because conforming to these conventions is part of the academic game they are learning to participate in.

Academic writing involves skills of analysis and the development of logical argument. These are skills which can be developed through training and practice. Such training requires feedback if it is to be effective, so procedures for peer and teacher feedback need to be provided. It is clear that fuzzy feedback is of limited use to writers (Hedgcock & Lefkowitz, 1994; Zamel, 1985), so both teachers and learners benefit from developing more focused feedback skills.

Talking about writing in the classroom plays an important role here (Weissberg, 1994). The use of check lists, peer response sheets and other types of guidance are useful ways of giving such talk a purpose. Discussion naturally leads to revision, either collaborative (Hedgcock & Lefkowitz, 1992) or individual. Indeed, it is only through successive revisions that writers can develop a piece of writing that will adequately communicate their meaning to an academic readership. Such revising is part of the responsibility which academic writers are assumed to have in relation to their readers. If the writer overburdens the reader with responsibility for negotiating meaning from their text, the piece of writing will be poorly evaluated.

Not surprisingly, task-based approaches are seen to be an important way of developing academic writing, particularly the kinds of reading, summarizing, synthesizing, and composing skills which are such a significant part of the typical academic writing assignment.

References

Braine, G. (1988). Commentary on Spack 1988. *TESOL Quarterly, 22,* 700–702.

Hedgcock, J., & Lefkowitz, N. (1992). Collaborative oral/aural revision in foreign language writing instruction. *Journal of Second Language Writing, 1,* 255–276.

Johns, A. M. (1988). Commentary on Spack 1988. *TESOL Quarterly, 22,* 705–707.

Spack, R. (1988). Initiating ESL students into the academic discourse community: How far should we go? *TESOL Quarterly, 22,* 29–51.

Weissberg, B. (1994) Speaking of writing: Some functions of talk in the ESL composition class. *Journal of Second Language Writing, 3,* 121–139.

Zamel, V. (1985) Responding to student writing. *TESOL Quarterly, 19,* 79–101.

◆ Paraphrasing and Summarizing

Recover the Text From the Questions

Levels
Any

Aims
Practice using linguistic
and other knowledge
cues in schema building

Class Time
20–40 minutes

Preparation Time
20 minutes

Resources
Text with 7–10
comprehension
questions, mostly
multiple-choice

Much writing involves developing a set of key ideas around a central theme. The following activity challenges writers to infer an author's organization or content schema from hints supplied in a set of questions and to write a text similar to one that they have not yet seen. This will encourage creative (but managed) writing, a change from traditional controlling/guiding frameworks.

Procedure

1. Choose a text written in a straightforward style, preferably one that comes with a set of multiple-choice questions.
2. Give each student a copy of the questions only. Do not give out the text at this point.
3. Have the students answer the questions without seeing the original text. Warn them that they must look for hints in the stems and alternatives and mobilize their world knowledge to help them answer.
4. Have the students try to write as much of the missing text as possible, recreating it from the cues in the questions and from their background knowledge.
5. Students can read each other's texts and should defend or query the various inventions that have been made.
6. Finally, hand out the original text so that the students can compare their versions with the author's.

Caveats and Options

1. Make sure the questions focus on important parts of the text.
2. Select material that reflects the level of your students.

3. Be ready to supply the first and/or last sentences of the text as further cues, if necessary.
4. Students can work individually or in groups.

Contributor

Alastair Allan has taught in Africa and Asia. He is a member of the English Department of the City University of Hong Kong. His interests include reading, writing, and language proficiency assessment.

Jigsaw Summary Writing

Levels
High intermediate +

Aims
Construct a coherent
summary

Class Time
90 minutes

Resources
Short articles from
popular science
magazines or from
professional or
academic journals (e.g.,
TESOL Quarterly or
TESOL Journal)
Overhead projector
(OHP) and supplies

This activity raises learners' awareness of the discourse structure of many academic texts. A jigsaw activity is used to focus learners' attention on a generally useful discourse structure, to allow collaboration within the text.

Procedure

1. Find several problem-solution texts. These may vary in length according to the level of the learners and their familiarity with the activity. I have used longer passages from advanced ESL reading books, and short, authentic articles from professional and academic journals. Magazines and serious newspapers might also be used as a source for texts.
2. Before class, cut the text up into sections. If possible, these sections should conform to the main problem-solution stages: Situation, Problem, Response(s), Result(s), Evaluation. Photocopy the initial stage and a later stage onto one sheet of paper. Make one copy for each group. Photocopy the other stages (preferably enlarged) onto one sheet of paper each.
3. To begin the session, divide the class into pairs or groups of three. One member of each group is the Writer and should remain seated at all times. The others are Reporters, and may move around the classroom. Give the Writers a copy of the initial and later stage of the text, and post the other stages in random order around the wall of the classroom.
4. The Writer begins by paraphrasing the initial and later stage of the text, and makes guesses about the missing content. The Reporters go back and forth from the Writer to the wall posters, orally reporting the main points contained there. Together, the members of the group collaborate to construct a summary of the complete text. The Writer eventually transfers this summary to the group's OHP transparency.

Different groups' versions of the text can then be compared and evaluated in a plenary feedback session. The teacher might also wish to write her own summary to add to the discussion.

Contributor

John Corbett lectures in the Department of English Language, University of Glasgow, Scotland.

Giving Students Authority

Levels
Advanced; college

Aims
Write a critical response to a reading in preparation for writing a research paper

Class Time
Two 50-minute class periods and out-of-class writing

Resources
Reading text
Handout (see Appendix)
Chalkboard

This activity gets ESL students to find out how much they know about a topic—by freewriting—before they read a related article. By becoming aware that a text is not just a store of information, students realize that they too are an authority on a subject.

The activity is a step in preparing university students to write a research paper. Summarizing skills are a useful component in teaching students to find and adapt an author's main ideas, which will then be used to support their own ideas. To enable students to do more than simply borrow someone else's ideas, guided questions ask students to reflect on what they read in light of their original freewriting on the topic. These reflections augment their written response.

Procedure

1. Introduce the topic of an article that will be handed out in class. Use an article that clearly takes one side of an issue and is relevant to the students' knowledge and experience. Ask the students questions to help them to find out how much they know about that topic and their attitudes toward it. Write their responses in note form on the chalkboard. Tell the students to copy this list and any more ideas that they think of on their own. Using their notes, the students then freewrite on the topic for approximately 30 minutes. Freewriting allows the students to brainstorm about the topic on paper; it is a way for them to record their thoughts. This initial written exploration of their ideas will enable the students to compare what they knew about the topic before reading with the new information and ideas they get after reading.

2. For homework, give the students an article that is related to the topic discussed in class. Their assignment is to read and write a summary

of the article. Ask them to take notes while they read it. Tell them that their notes should only be on parts of the text that are important to them, for example, new words, ideas that they agreed/disagreed with, parts that they couldn't understand, interesting/new pieces of information.

3. In a subsequent class, ask the students to tell you the main ideas of the article and any key words that they needed to use in their summaries. Ask them to distinguish between supporting ideas and main ideas. As a class, discuss any inconsistencies in the students' decisions about what is important enough to include in the summary. Also, use this time to answer any questions that they may have about vocabulary or ideas in the text that were not clear to them.

4. Next, ask the students to write a personal response to the article. Give them the list of questions below. These are meant to guide (not prescribe) their response: Tell them to answer only the questions that apply to them. Encourage the students to ask/answer any more questions that they may have. To help generate their responses, remind them to refer back to their original freewriting, the article that they read, and their notes.

5. A follow up to this lesson can include a class discussion about the different responses that each student had toward the article. Reassure them (if necessary) that there are many correct responses and encourage them to express what prompted their particular responses to the article based on their own knowledge and experience.

6. As an initial step toward writing a research paper that the students will write as a course requirement, assign this activity again. However, this time, the students select their own topic and an article that relates to their specific topic.

Caveats and Options

1. It is necessary to have introduced and practiced summary skills prior to doing this activity.

2. For large classes (more than 25 students), divide students into groups and assign three or four different texts, all related to the same topic, to each group. All the steps remain the same except that instead of a group discussion, the students read summaries that the individuals

in the other groups produced. The students choose a new article based on a summary that interests them and write their own response to it. Later, the two responses can be compared.

References and Further Reading

Reid, J. (1993). Historical perspectives on writing and reading in the ESL classroom. In J. G. Carson & I. Leki (Eds.), *Reading in the composition classroom: Second language perspectives* (pp. 33–60). Boston, MA: Heinle & Heinle.

Zamel, V. (1992). Writing one's way into reading. *TESOL Quarterly, 26*, 463–485.

Appendix: Sample Response Question Handout

1. Think about what your original ideas about the topic were and how they may have changed or expanded.
2. Think about the differences, similarities, and questions between your original thoughts and ideas and your new ideas after reading the article.

- Which of your ideas were similar to information you found in the article?
- What new ideas did you get after reading the article?
- What in the article didn't you understand?
- Which things from the article do you want to know more about?
- Which parts of the article did you disagree with?
- What, if anything, would you like to ask or say to the author?

Contributor

Randall L. Cotten is an instructor at Saint Mary College, Nagoya, Japan.

Diagramming Before Summarizing

Levels
High intermediate +

Aims
Identify main ideas from
a chapter and present
them in writing

Class Time
Three class periods

Resources
Academic textbook
chapter from a subject
such as business,
psychology, or
communication

Building skills in writing summaries is important preparation for study at many universities. Students enrolled in university classes are usually required to read a textbook for each class. Writing summaries about chapters they have read is one way students can review course content. Sometimes students are required to turn in textbook chapter summaries as a course requirement.

Procedure

1. Introduce the task: Students will be writing a one- to two-page summary from a chapter of an academic textbook.
2. Ask students to state the characteristics of a good summary. List the characteristics on the chalkboard. Remind students to try to apply many of these characteristics when writing their summaries.
3. Hand out the textbook chapters and have students skim the chapter by focusing on the title, subtitles, and introductory part. Ask students to make a diagram showing the main parts in the chapter. (See sample below.)

**Controlling
Idea**

Part I   Part II   Part III

main
ideas   main
ideas   main
ideas

Ask students to skim the chapter a second time looking for the main ideas for each part of the chapter. They can add these main ideas to their diagram. When adding notes to their diagram, it is best to write key words or phrases, not whole sentences.

4. Ask students to put the textbook chapter away and only use their diagram to write their summary. When writing their summary, students can introduce the author's name and the title of the chapter and book in the opening sentence. Students should state the thesis of the chapter in the first part of their summary. Then students can write a few sentences about each part of the chapter.

5. Ask students to get into groups of three to peer edit their classmates' summaries. Give students peer editing questions such as the following:

- What characteristics of good summaries does this student writer apply very effectively? Try to be specific in your praise.
- What characteristics of good summaries could this student writer improve? Try to be specific in your comments.

6. Ask students to rewrite their summary, incorporating suggestions from their peer editors. In addition, when rewriting, they should try to use their own ideas to improve it.

Caveats and Options

You may want to write the peer editing questions on a handout.

References and Further Reading

Lipp, E. (1990). *From paragraph to term paper: A reading and composition text for advanced students*. New York: Heinle & Heinle.

Contributor

Ellen Lipp is Associate Professor in the Department of Linguistics at California State University, Fresno, in the United States.

In Other Words

Levels
High intermediate +

Aims
Practice academic
writing tasks in an
integrated way

Class Time
60–80 minutes

Resources
Worksheet (see
Appendix)

This activity integrates practice in several academic writing tasks into a single activity based on a brief text and makes students aware of the similarities between the tasks and of certain uses of parallelism.

Procedure

1. Begin by discussing assignments in other courses that will require the skills of paraphrasing, summarizing, and outlining. Introduce the activity and distribute the worksheets.
2. Have students skim the text for the thesis and main ideas and write them on the worksheet.
3. Listen to two or three students' theses and main ideas. Write correct ones on the board, listing main points one under another. Ask the students to help make the list parallel in structure. Discuss the position of these elements in the essay and in paragraphs. Point out the sequence of transitions used to introduce the main ideas.
4. Review the requirements for paraphrasing (i.e., include all the information; do not change the meaning; change the wording; change the sentence structures; do not change the order).
5. Ask a few students to write their paraphrases on the board; then discuss them.
6. Review the requirements for summarizing (i.e., include only the main points plus all the requirements for paraphrasing). Point out, either before or after students write summaries (Step 4), that everything they need they already have in Questions 2 and 3 on the worksheet.
7. Ask some students to read their summaries aloud after which the others can critique them.
8. Have students do Question 5, a one-sentence summary. Volunteers write theirs on the board. Point out the need for parallelism.

9. As students complete the outline individually have them compare their work in pairs or small groups.

Appendix: Sample Worksheet on Paraphrasing, Summarizing, and Outlining

Directions: Quickly skim the text below to find the thesis and the main ideas or points. Underline them. When you have finished, we will do the exercises below.

Body Motion and Communication

Human beings communicate both verbally, with words, and nonverbally. To understand what a person is saying, we need to comprehend not only his or her words but also the messages being sent in other ways. An important type of nonverbal communication is body motion.

One form of body motion is movement of the body and of parts of the body. People from different cultures may move their bodies in different ways. An analysis of folk dance styles suggests that people tend to fall into one of two groups—those who move the trunk of the body as if it were a solid, one-unit block, and those who move it as if it were two or more units—bending and swaying the different sections independently of each other.

Another form of body motion is walking style. Differences in walking styles are so marked that it has been claimed that Frenchmen can recognize an American from 200 yards away simply by the way the American walks. To the French eye, the American walk is uncivilized. Interestingly, many Puerto Ricans have a very different perception of how Americans walk; they think have an uptight, authoritarian walk. It may well be that these Puerto Ricans' perception of the American gait is colored due to the political status of Puerto Rico and because of the role many Americans play there—a dominant, superordinate role. In any event, there is probably as much variation in walking style among the members of any given culture as there is between two cultures.

A third form of body motion is rhythm. Recent studies of rhythm as it relates to body movements have revealed new insights into human communication. When a person talks, movements of the fingers, eyelids and eyebrows, head, and other body parts occur as a sort of rhythmic accompaniment to the rise and fall of the voice and the flow of syllables. The whole body moves "in sync" with the words. Not only are people in sync with themselves, but as two people converse, their body movements gradually fall into rhythmic harmony. When synchrony does not occur between speakers, it is usually a sign of underlying tension.

1. Copy the thesis:

List the main points (do not write complete sentences):

-
-
-

2. Paraphrase the thesis:

-
-
-

3. Paraphrase the first sentences of the last three paragraphs:

-
-
-

4. Write a summary of the whole text in four sentences:
5. Write a one-sentence summary of the text:
6. Complete the outline on the next page; be sure to use parallel structures:

Body Motion and Communication

Thesis: An important type of nonverbal communication is body motion.
  I. Movements of the body and body parts
     A. One-unit cultures
     B.

II. Walking styles
  A. Culturally based interpretations of American walking style
    1.
    2.
  B.
III.
  A. Synchrony of sound and body
  B.
    1. Harmony
    2.

Contributor

Sylvia Mulling teaches ESL at Kean College, New Jersey, in the United States.

A Summary Response

Levels
High intermediate +

Aims
Learn to paraphrase and summarize
Learn new invention strategies
Build schema for a producing written language on a given topic in an argumentative essay

Class Time
30 minutes–1 hour

Resources
Copies of an article

This activity is a variation on a technique that has been successfully used by many instructors in writing and reading classes in the ESL program at Georgia State University.

Procedure

1. Elicit topics of interest from students and find an appropriate article on one of these topics.
2. Copy and distribute the article to the students.
3. As a homework assignment, each student reads the article and writes a summary and a response based upon his or her reaction. The response answers the following questions: Do you agree or disagree with opinions of the author? What are your reasons for agreeing or disagreeing?
4. Initiate a class discussion of the article.
5. Students compare their summaries and share their responses in small groups.

Caveats and Options

1. Use student summaries to illustrate paraphrasing techniques: synonyms, antonyms and negation, varying word order, and substituting complex, compound, and simple sentence structure.
2. Students can write thesis statements based upon their responses and argumentative essays based on their thesis statements.
3. Students can write a summary/response after watching a video in class, a commercial, or political advertisements.

Contributors

Karen Peterson is an ESL instructor at Georgia State University. She has a Master of Science in Applied Linguistics. Michele Kilgore is an ESL instructor at Georgia State University. She has a Master of Science in Applied Linguistics and is working on her doctorate.

◆ Synthesizing
Summary-Response Writing

Levels
High intermediate +

Aims
Extract salient facts and statements from published sources and incorporate these in academic essays

Class Time
Several 45–50 minute periods

Resources
One or more published articles on a topic of interest to students
Lists of useful vocabulary (see Appendix)

R ecent research shows the interactive nature of reading and writing in both L1 and L2 language learning. This technique teaches students to focus on and restate key points in a published text, to find parallels in their own knowledge and other readings, and to critique the text.

Procedure

1. Select one article that is relevant to the students' goals and interests. The article should be on a topic of some complexity or controversy— anything worthy of further discussion will do. If prereading and vocabulary activities are needed, carry these out before assigning students to read the article on their own. If desired, lead an in-class discussion of the content of the article after students have read it to prepare them for the following work; for more advanced students or a class that has selected different articles to read, this step may not be appropriate.

2. Explain to students that they will write a brief summary to highlight key points in the article. In this portion of the assignment, they will

   - learn to cite portions of text directly and to paraphrase text
   - search their memories to find other bits of knowledge, experiences, or prior readings of which the current article reminds them
   - describe and discuss these connections, explaining why they are similar to or reminiscent of the text
   - write a paragraph to express their own opinions about the text, including evaluations and/or suggestions for action or change.

3. Select a manageable chunk of text: the opening paragraph, perhaps, or first section of the article. Have students underline or copy key

phrases and sentences from the text, noting the relationships of the ideas expressed. Make sure they look up words they don't know.

4. Have them write one or two sentences that they believe express the main idea of each paragraph in the chunk. Encourage them to alter the wording of the sentence so they are not using direct quotes, except in the case of unique terms or phrases.

5. Either have several volunteers put their sentences on the board for full-class discussion or put students in groups to compare their sentences. In either case, the goal for students is to look at the alternatives, decide what's effective and what isn't, and come up with a revised statement of the main idea. This step can be repeated with other chunks or the teacher can generate several alternatives for the existing material. Examples of good summary statements should demonstrate use of metalanguage, quotation marks for cited material, and paraphrasing to shorten or restate an idea.

6. Assign students the task of writing a short summary of the article during the remainder of the class or for homework.

7. Have students form discussion groups to talk over the content of the article. Tell them to describe or explain to their classmates some other experience or reading that the current article has made them recall.

8. After they've had time to explore these connections, ask students to share their opinions about the content of the article. Encourage disagreement; it stimulates further reflection. Insist, however, that their stated opinions be grounded in reliable sources, not hearsay or speculation.

9. In class or as homework, have students write one or more paragraphs to explain what they've discussed in Steps 7 and 8 above. (See list of useful phrases in the Appendix.) These should be combined with the summary from the preceding day and turned in to the teacher for comments and corrections.

10. At this point, terminate the activity or repeat it with a different reading selection. Students can also share their written drafts with classmates for further discussion of effective writing skills.

Caveats and Options

1. Use the existing drafts to have students write a formal essay or research paper. This is accomplished by turning the summary-response on its head: from the Personal Opinion segment, the student identifies a potential thesis for the essay, and from the Connections and Summary segments, he finds support for the thesis. The work now continues as in any advanced essay class, but with a head start on the content of the essay. I find this to be a very useful technique for showing students what's meant by *explicit and concrete detail.*

2. The activity could be adapted for low-level students by selecting an appropriate text, such as narrative or descriptive writing; this could also be a useful technique for literary analysis of poetry, short stories, and novels, and could be used in low level classes for this purpose.

Appendix: Sample Lists

It is always helpful to give students a starter list of structural forms to help them get started. Here are some possibilities, but teachers will want to modify the list to suit their students' skills and course goals:

Useful Phrases for Writing Summaries and Paraphrases
  In this article [about _____] the author asserts, " . . . "
  In this article [about _____] the author asserts that . . . .
    (alternate verbs: states, claims, declares, insists, holds, says)
  The thesis of this article is [that] . . .
    (alternate nouns: main point, main idea, central theme)
  According to the writer, . . .
  In the writer's opinion, . . .
  Based on his/her research, the writer believes that . . .
  The author says, " . . . " In other words, . . . /To state this differently,
  . . . /The author thus claims that . . .

Useful Phrases for Making Connections:
  The ideas in this article remind me of. . . /recall . . .
  This brings to mind another article by . . .
  When I read this article, I thought about . . .
  As I considered the author's argument, an old story/incident/event came to mind.

A similar idea is expressed by _____ in (title of book, story, etc.)
The author's story is reminiscent of another event which occurred . . .

Useful Phrases for Stating Opinions/Critiques:

To express agreement:
   The author's arguments are persuasive/compelling/well-founded.
   I agree with the author's views about . . .
   The assertions in this article are, in my opinion, correct.

To express disagreement:
   The author's arguments are unconvincing/weak/faulty/inadequate.
   I disagree with the author's views about . . .
   The assertions in this article are, in my opinion, incorrect.

Contributor

Alice Gertzman is a graduate student in the Department of Linguistics and Modern English Language at Lancaster University in the United Kingdom.

Please Take Note

Levels
Intermediate +

Aims
Draw relevant
information together
from several sources

Class Time
40 minutes–1 hour

Resources
Realia on a topic (e.g.,
environmental issues,
animal rights,
euthanasia) from
several sources
Essay question
Overhead projector
(OHP) and supplies

This activity develops synthesis skills using a number of sources. Note-taking practice enhances the skill of choosing relevant material. Organizing these notes into a coherent response to the assigned question should result in good paragraph development. The same process can be expanded to a complete essay.

Procedure

1. Cull materials from what comes onto your doormat: handbills, periodic reports from Greenpeace, Amnesty, charities, supermarkets; arrange these as a packet for the students to read.
2. Prepare a question (or give an essay title) that can be answered from the collected texts.
3. As the students take notes, move around the class to be sure that they are learning how to take relevant notes (guard against copying or memorizing sentences).
4. When the first students has finished her paragraph ask him or her to write it on a transparency or on the board.
5. As each student completes her paragraph, ask her to write it up.
6. Everyone is invited to look at the paragraphs and offer constructive criticism (i.e., edit them). (This activity makes good use of quick students' time. Slower students may edit only one piece.) Students learn to spot and correct errors.
7. As you move around the classroom, try to glean: (a) problems with selecting relevant points; (b) grammar points widely misunderstood; (c) problems in paragraphing shared by a number of students. Following Step 6, you can take up these three points with the whole class.

8. Clean copies of the paragraph should be handed in and a homework assignment with similar requirements should be given for further practice.

Contributor

Norma Green is Senior Tutor in the English Language Unit, University of Wales Aberystwyth, in the United Kingdom.

Computer Conferencing

Levels
Advanced

Aims
Argue, compare and
contrast, express
opinions, (dis)agree,
formulate and develop
ideas

Class Time
Two essay writing
cycles/semester and two
e-mail comments/week

Resources
Lectures and required
readings on a content-
area course

The following suggestions are based on an experiment in which nonreal-time computer conferencing was used to introduce students to the idea of writing as a process, and for discussing relevant topics in writing. The suggestions lend themselves to adaptions depending on the number of students, their language skills, time, and computer technology available.

Procedure

1. Set up a computer-conferencing system so that students have access to computer terminals or microcomputers that are hooked up with the college's/university's host computer (or if they are off campus, that they have microcomputers and a modem to contact the computer, see Appendix A).
2. For sending off and replying to messages have, for example, a VAX or SUN electronic mail system available as well as, for example, an Emacs text processing program.
3. Organize a 2-hour training session so that students get familiar with these systems and the basic commands.
4. Have students write an outline for an essay on an agreed topic and submit hard copies to each other and you.
5. Students give feedback on outlines by computer-conferencing with each other and you, a native speaker of English.
6. Ask students to compose their essays based on this feedback and submit hardcopies to one another and you.
7. Students give feedback on the first versions of the essays by computer-conferencing. Students can be provided with a checklist to make sure they will look at the draft from a number of perspectives—spelling, grammar, discourse, content—adapting ideas from introductions to process writing, for example, Reid (1988).

8. Students revise their essays and finally submit the second version (together with the final outline) to you for grading.
9. Repeat the steps for the second essay of the semester.
10. After having listened to lectures and/or studied required readings, students discuss relevant topics by computer-conferencing with each other and you. This is a way to introduce students to interactive writing in a computer conferencing context, to increase student "talking time" and thus also their responsibility in conducting discussions.
11. Initiate the discussion of the week, for example, in the form of a question.
12. Tell students they may answer the question or comment on the topic in any way they wish.
13. Have everyone read each other's comments and respond to them, by for example agreeing or disagreeing. They are to mail a minimum of two e-mail messages per week.
14. Repeat the steps for any number of topics.

References and Further Reading

Reid, J. M. (1988). *The process of composition*. Englewood Cliffs, NJ: Prentice Hall Regents.

**Appendix A:
Computer
Conferencing
System Used
in
Experiment**

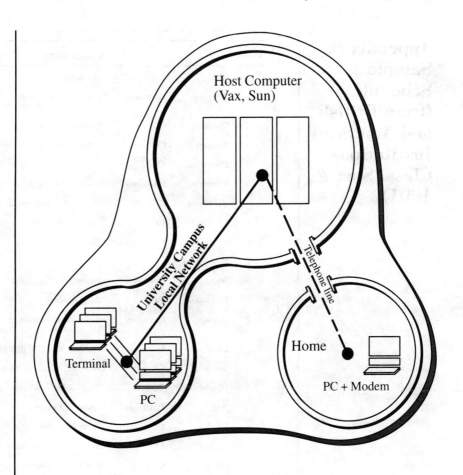

Host Computer
(Vax, Sun)

University Campus
Local Network

Telephone line

Terminal

PC

Home

PC + Modem

Appendix B: Sample Schedule (from British and American Institutions Class, Spring 1991)

Week			Assignment
1	**Class**		Introduction, Pretest
2	Writing	**Hardcopy**	Initial outline for Essay 1 "The role of the Constitution in the U.S.A. and Finland"
	Discussion	**CC**	"The constitution and social realities"
3	Writing	**CC**	Comments on initial outline for Essay 1
	Discussion	**CC**	"Ireland"
4	Writing	**Hardcopy**	Version 1 of Essay 1
	Discussion	**CC**	"The effect of Thatcherism on politics"
5	Writing	**CC**	Comments on Version 1 of Essay 1
	Discussion	**CC**	"The American class system"
6	No assignment		
7	Writing	**Hardcopy**	Version 2 of Essay 1 and final outline
	Discussion	**CC**	"Demographics"
8	Writing	**Hardcopy**	Initial outline for Essay 2 "The effect of American icons on Finnish culture"
	Discussion	**CC**	"The American civil rights movement"
9	Writing	**CC**	Comments on initial outline for Essay 2
	Discussion	**CC**	"Race relations and ethnic groups in Britain"
10	Writing	**Hardcopy**	Version 1 of Essay 2
	Discussion	**CC**	"North American Indians"
11	Writing	**CC**	Comments on Version 2 of Essay 2
	Discussion	**CC**	"U.S. foreign policy"
12	No assignment		
13	Writing	**Hardcopy**	Version 2 of Essay 2 and final outline
	Discussion	**CC**	"The effect of Thatcherism on culture and the Arts"
14	**Class**		Posttest

[1] CC stands for computer conferencing.

Appendix C: Sample E-mail Messages (unedited)

Hello

I'm afraid I don't have anything exciting to say about the writings. This is not to say that they weren't interesting. I enjoyed reading them, but they were quite similar again.

Maija has been in a hurry when writing the essay, I suppose. It was rather short and the spelling was not so correct. Otherwise it was good.

Reijo had a lot of his own opinions in the essay, that's interesting. But I don't agree with him about the huge popularity" of American football. The paragraphs and their order (??) is clear.

Kaija is clear and bright, as usual. She seens to have knowledge about the subject. There's many good sharp comments and good conclusions in the essay and it is quite long as you can see.

Taija has written a good, long essay as well. But what do you mean by judging a couintry by appearance. Aren't buildings etc. culture, too? Maybe you could explain that a bit clearer. or something.

Gotta go now. Bye.

Saija

– Good day,

I was just wondering whether we're going to write on Indians or not? Or do we have another free week again? It wouldn't bother me if we did? But on the other hand I think Mr Brown did it again, and I think we could find something to say about this issue.

It was rather interesting when we compared Indian-American problems to our Lapp-Finn-Swedish-problems. But I think that it is right that these people have some rights, after all they were there before us or the discoverers of America. I know you probably think now that if I lived in the North and did not have the same rights as the Lapps I would be angry, just like many Americans must be, at least that's what our dear lecturer said. But still I think that both we and they owe a lot to these "people of nature" after taking their land and properties.

Now I started wondering why did I put the Swedish-problem there, but then, there are a lot of Finns who see Swedish speaking people as some kind of a threat. But then again, they have been here for centuries now, we should be proud of the cultural variety they have brought here. But because we Finns are so jealous of everything, and that's why Finns dislike their Swedish speaking minority so much, we want them out of here. Why did I say jealous? Well, in general this little minority is agroup of quite wealthy and well educated people who have a lot of power in their hands. And of course this is too much for ordinary Finns.

Of course this is not the case with the Indians, I think the general public in the USA considers Indians still lazy and stupid natives who have to be taken care of by the wise and civilized white man.

Now I just lost my thoughts and cant find them anywhere so I'll say bye for now.

Kaija

Contributors

Paula Kalaja and Sirpa Leppänen teach in the Department of English, University of Jyväskylä, Finland.

Coffee, Tea, or Karma Anyone?

Levels
Low intermediate +;
college

Aims
Determine relationships
among pieces of
information
Organize ideas
persuasively
Format the text to suit
the intended readers

Class Time
8–9 hours over 2
weeks, not necessarily
consecutive days

Resources
Worksheets, maps, or
flowcharts (teacher-
made)
Data from appropriate
reference sources (e.g.,
dictionary, almanac,
factbook, encyclopedia)

This writing project introduces students to the rudiments of analyzing information for, drafting, and revising an academic essay on how words, particularly international ones, have entered English and their own languages. Although ostensibly an arcane choice of topic, the immigration and emigration of vocabulary is an interesting way for students to revisit the historical interrelations among their cultures and countries and to pick up new words related to their fields.

Procedure

1. Create a list of English words and etymologies. A sensible selection of words would come from vocabulary connected to the students' disciplines and derived from their languages. The list should also include words that have entered English in a variety of ways: through trade, political or religious influence, cultural or scientific exchange, or neologism, for example. (See Appendix for sample list.)
2. Ask students to examine the list and hypothesize about how the words might have entered English. As their discussion crests, have them make sentences that reflect the observations of the class.
3. Develop a map or flowchart of categories of entrance processes for English words. (See sample on next page.)

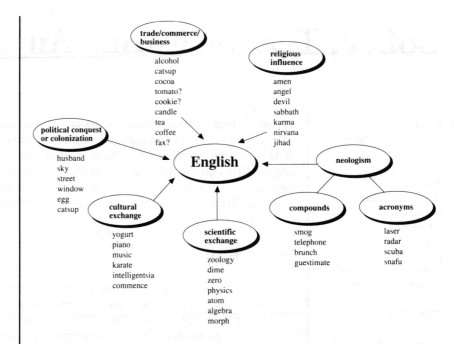

4. As students contribute categories or vocabulary, refine the flowchart or map.
5. As a group, develop sample controlling ideas and introductory paragraphs. Have the class experiment with many possible introductions, eliciting as many different possibilities as you have time for so that everyone must contribute and not just copy the ideas of their classmates.

If the class is interested, you may want to give them a copy of the Indo-European language tree (see, e.g., Pei, 1976) or a chart of the world language classifications (see, e.g., Katzner, 1986). They don't need this information to write the essay, but it will make the relationships among languages explicit and suggest that etymology and semantics aren't just guessing—philologists and linguists have been systematically analyzing what and why words mean for hundreds of years.

6. Help the class use the map or flowchart to organize the essay.
7. Use your favorite revision procedures to help students refine their drafts. Because students have created the essay in collaborative groups, peer revision works well as a first step.
8. If your program has a student newsletter, as a final step, you may want to ask several students to rework the class's conclusions as an article for publication. Their audience will be different (i.e., the general student population vs. the teacher and themselves), so they will have to refocus their presentation slightly—good practice, even for newer writers.

Caveats and Options

1. No matter how carefully crafted a writing task is, no matter how sensitively chosen its topics or readings, it is unlikely that the task will suit the tastes and academic objectives of every group of students (assuming, of course, that texts are available and that students can afford them). Writing projects (such as this one on etymology) tailored to the requirements of particular groups of students can better help them learn to write to the specifications of their intended post-ESOL destination. Such projects need not be unrealistically time consuming to produce or administer and can be revised and recycled as appropriate. They can also provide a realistic alternative to costly books for instructors or students without institutional support.
2. Instructors with access to the reference department of a library can use such projects to generate interest in how to do basic library research.
3. Instructors without such access and, possibly, without budgets to purchase many materials, may want to develop personal reference collections of almanacs, world or local factbooks, catalogues, and the like—versatile reference works with long shelf lives.

References and Further Reading

Katzner, K. (1986). *The languages of the world*. London: Routledge & Kegan Paul.

Pei, M. (1976). *The story of Latin and the romance languages*. New York: Harper & Row.

Webster's Third New International Dictionary.

Acknowledgment

I acknowledge the contributions of Nancy Overman to another version of this activity.

Appendix: Sample Word List

How Might These Words Have Entered English?

1. alcohol [Sp. fr. Ar *al-kuhl* (powdered antimony)]
2. amen [L fr. Gk fr. Heb]
3. catsup/ketchup [Malay *kechap* (spiced fish sauce)]
4. coffee [It fr. Turk fr. Ar *qahwah*]
5. cotton [F fr. Ar *qutn*]
6. hamburger [G]
7. intelligentsia [Russ]
8. karate [Jap]
9. laser [fr. *l*ight *a*mplification by *s*timulated *e*mission of *r*adiation]
10. music [It]
11. smog [fr. *sm*oke and f*og*]
12. sugar [F fr. L fr. Ar fr. Per fr. Skt *sarkara* (pebble)]
13. tea [Chin *cha'a*]
14. window [fr. ON *vindauga* (wind/eye)]
15. zero [F fr. It fr. L fr. Ar *sifr* (empty, cipher, zero)]

Key to language abbreviations: Ar = Arabic; Chin = Chinese; F = French; G = German; Gk = Greek; Heb = Hebrew; It = Italian; Jap = Japanese; L = Latin; ON = Old Norse; Per = Persian; Russ = Russian; Skt = Sanskrit; Sp = Spanish; Turk = Turkish

Contributor

Marilyn Kupetz is Assistant Editor of TESOL Journal *and* TESOL Quarterly.

Using the Press to Teach Writing

Levels
Intermediate +

Aims
Develop a contrastive
essay using real material

Class Time
30–45 minutes

Preparation Time
10 minutes or less

Resources
Newspaper ads for
vacation rentals
Equipment to reproduce
the advertisements
Handout (see
Appendix)

A balance can be achieved between control and creativity in order to allow students the freedom to express themselves without becoming lost in a maze of structures and vocabulary beyond their comprehension. This activity has controlled content but allows some freedom of expression and can be considered an attempt at communicating a meaningful message from the writer to the reader.

Procedure

1. Have students use the travel section of the newspaper (or other source) and choose four or more resorts that they would like to visit.

Appendix: Sample Vacation Time Activities Handout

No. 1 The Falls Apts. Clean, beautiful efficiencies, near beach. All two br, a/c, pool. $250/week + utilities $50 dep.

No. 2 This month only! Sandy Hotel special! Only $25/day weekly rate (single). Tennis courts $15 each additional.

No. 3 Ritz Hotel. 2 mi from beach. All rooms $55/day. Stay M-F Sat and Sun Free. Pool, Tennis, 4 star rest.

No. 4 The Waves on the Beach. $45/day single (ocean view slightly higher) Weekender special—stay Sat. Sun. Free.

Warm up and Prewriting

1. Which resort is definitely on the beach?

   _____

2. Does the Sandy Hotel have a restaurant?

   _____

3. How much would it cost for two people to spend a week at the Sandy Hotel?

   _____

4. How much would it cost to stay Monday through Sunday at The Ritz?

   _____

5. Is there a disadvantage to staying at the Ritz?

   _____

6. Can you tell from the advertisement what the double rate is at the Waves?

   _____

7. Which is better, a week at the Ritz including the weekend, or a week at the Falls Apartments?

   _____

Major Topic: Which resort would you choose and why? Compare and contrast the possible choices listing the advantages and disadvantages of each before coming to your own conclusion.

For my vacation, I would prefer to go to the _____ and spend _____ (days, weeks) since this resort . . . .

_____

_____

_____

_____

_____

Caveats and Options

Students may do a similar exercise by writing from an outline (see sample on next page).

City by Night

A: Expectations: (positive side)
1. Comfortable limousine for transport
2. Elegant dining room
3. Expensive dinner
4. First class show
5. A famous band

B: What really happened (negative side)
1. Old bus picked us up late
2. Dining room dirty, too hot
3. Dinner was stale chicken
4. Show had no class
5. Band was unknown, couldn't play

When we signed up for the City by Night Tour during our vacation in Metro last year, we were expecting an exciting night on the town and first rate entertainment. The ad promised a comfortable limousine. However, the promised limousine was an old noisy bus that arrived thirty minutes late to take us to the City Lights Club for our evening.

In conclusion, we paid $75 per person for an unpleasant experience that was worth only about $5.95.

Now using the models, write your own essay about an experience that you did not expect.

2. Students learn strategies for collecting and interpreting information and putting it together in a coherent whole. Other authentic language material can be accessed and adapted by an innovative teacher. Guidebooks, available from auto clubs, advertisements and writings by regular English students all make good sources. These can be rephrased and shortened to fit a particular class. The main point in these examples is for the instructor to create a realistic purpose for the writers. (Dvorak, 1986)
3. Teachers need to address both the surface-level language-related problems and the deeper areas of meaning in teaching the writing skill

without overloading the students with too many rules or allowing them to write extensive error-filled passages without any guidelines.

References and Further Reading

Dvorak, T. (1986). Writing in the foreign language. In B. H. Wing (Ed.), *Listening, reading and writing: Analysis and application.* Middlebury, VT: Northeast Conference.

Krashen, S. D., & Terrell, T. D. (1983). *The natural approach.* Oxford: Pergamon.

Shih, M. (1986, December). Content-based approaches to teaching academic writing. *TESOL Quarterly, 20,* 617–648.

Contributor

Douglas R. Magrath teaches ESL at Seminole Community College. He has also provided ESL workshops for Volusia County, Florida, and presented at local and regional TESOL meetings. He has published in Foreign Language Annals, Selected Articles from the TESOL Newsletter, *and* Teaching English to Deaf and Second Language Students. *He also trains teachers for Volusia County, Florida.*

Using L1 Composition in an L2 Writing Class

Levels
High intermediate

Aims
Respond to writing
without automatically
focusing on error
Learn to look beyond
surface characteristics of
writing to evaluate and
revise it

Class Time
Several 50-minute
periods

Resources
Student survey form
(see Appendix A)
Interview assignment
sheet (see Appendix B)
Questions for guided
oral report (see
Appendix C)

Although deflecting attention from error is difficult, one way to accomplish this is for teachers to spend time working with students' L1 writing. Such an approach is relevant to the ESOL writing class because, in recent years, research has begun to demonstrate a deeper relationship between L1 and L2 writing than the relationship of interference presupposed by the contrastive rhetoric hypothesis. Little has been done, however, to apply these findings to problems of response to student writing in the classroom. This activity encourages students and teachers in these directions.

Procedure

The Survey (Class Period 1)

1. Students fill out anonymous survey forms to answer questions on their writing practices. The purpose is to get them to begin to think of themselves as writers in two languages. A sample survey form, with one student's replies, is included in Appendix A. The responses shown are typical and reveal a difference in degree of confidence in the strength of L1 versus L2 written expression.

The Interview (Homework Assignment and Class Period 2)

1. Have students look beyond themselves to the writing of others, with each student using the interview assignment sheet to interview two people, one who writes frequently in the student's L1 and one who writes frequently in English (see Harris, 1984).
2. Have each student present and compare responses in the form of a 200- to 250-word summary.

3. In class, use reports of comments as a springboard for discussion of the writing process, including the procedures followed and the importance of revision.

The Composition (Homework Assignment)

1. Ask each student to write a composition in his or her L1 on an assigned topic. You will end up with a packet of compositions written in a variety of languages.
2. Collect the compositions, then duplicate and distribute them to the class.

The Oral Presentation (Class Period 3)

1. Have students present their compositions to the class orally. Cultural show-and-tell is a familiar tradition in ESOL, and it is here extended to the writing class as students are given a set of questions to use as a guide (see next section) and asked to explain their compositions. The use of guided questions is important, because without them, students may misunderstand what is wanted and simply try to translate their compositions literally into English. Because the focus of the exercise is the writing process, do not permit students to translate beyond an occasional phrase that a student author may be especially pleased with and particularly wish to share with the class. Instead, have students tell about their compositions by paraphrasing and discussing.
2. After each oral presentation, give the rest of the class an opportunity to ask questions and offer suggestions. Although at the beginning, students' questions may respond exclusively to the content (*Where are you from?* or *Now that you're studying here, do you still think that it is the best?*), gradually they begin to ask about and comment on other aspects of the writing as well (*Why is your third paragraph so long?* or *I didn't understand his composition; he could be more expressive about it*). You should model the role of peer evaluator and then use students' comments to further draw their attention to various aspects of the writing process and to characteristics of good writing.

References and Further Reading

Cumming, A. (1989). Writing expertise and second language proficiency. *Language Learning, 39*, 81–141.

Dawe, C. W., & Dornan, E. A. (1984). *One to one: Resources for conference-centered writing* (2nd ed.). Boston: Little, Brown.

Edelsky, C. (1982). Writing in a bilingual program: The relation of L1 and L2 texts. *TESOL Quarterly, 16*, 211–228.

Harris, M. (1984). *Practice for a purpose*. Boston: Houghton-Mifflin.

Hottel-Burkhart, N. (1982). *Research in L2 composition: The importance of L1 data*. Paper presented at the 16th Annual TESOL Convention, Honolulu, Hawaii.

Leung, L. (1984). The relationship between L1 and L2 writing. *Language Learning and Communication, 3*, 187–202.

Zamel, V. (1985). Responding to student writing. *TESOL Quarterly, 19*, 75–101.

Appendix A: Sample Student Survey Form

Sample, unedited answers are filled in.

1. What strong points does your writing have, in your opinion?

   English writing: None
   Native language writing: wide vocebulery, good knowledge of gramme, feeling of language

2. What weak points does your writing have, in your opinion?

   English writing: small vocebulery, little knowledge of English gramme
   Native language writing: Long way to get to the point.

3. Do you think you succeed in getting across everything you intend to say when you write?

   English writing: not always
   Native language writing: not always

4. Do you use a dictionary while you are writing?

   English writing: Yes, very often
   Native language writing: very seldom

5. Do you think about grammar when you write?

English writing: Yes
Native language writing: No

6. Do you take some brief notes before starting to write?

English writing: Sometimes I'm taking brief notes
Native language writing: (same)

7. While you are writing, do you think about the reader who is going to be reading your writing?

English writing: always
Native language writing: (same)

Appendix B: Interview Assignment Sheet

Find someone who writes often in your L1, and interview the person about his or her writing. Here are some questions which you might ask:

How much and what do you write?
How long does it take you to finish writing something?
Do you follow any steps when you write? If so, what are they?
Do you ever get stuck in the middle of a piece of writing? If so, what do you do?
After you finish a piece of writing, do you revise it?
In your opinion, what characteristics should good writing have?

Write a paragraph in which you summarize the results of the interview.

Now, find a native English speaker who writes often in English, and interview this person the same way. Again, write a paragraph in which you summarize the results.

Appendix C: Questions for Guided Oral Report

1. In what language was the paper written?
2. The topic of the paper was why you decided to come to Central.

   What reasons did you give? How did you decide what to include in the paper? Is there anything you were originally going to include, but decided later to leave out? Why?

3. Did you find any part of the paper especially difficult to write? What was so difficult about it? How did you solve the problem?
4. In what order did you arrange the reasons you gave in the paper? Why did you decide to arrange them that way? Is there any relationship between the way you arranged the reasons and the way you divided the paper into paragraphs? (Questions 2 and 4 should be adapted to fit the assigned topic and writing purpose. Here, students had been assigned to write a causal analysis essay on the topic stated.)
5. How did you conclude the paper?
6. Do you think this paper would be different if you had written in English instead? How would it be different?
7. Now that you've had a chance to look at the paper again, is there anything you would change if you rewrote it?

Contributor

Andrea G. Osburne teaches in the Department of English, Central Connecticut State University, in the United States.

Getting Together

Levels
Intermediate +

Aims
Discuss and show the
pros and cons of a topic

Class Time
40–50 minutes

Resources
Collection of arguments
for and against a
controversial statement

This activity helps students produce an essay as a follow-up activity to
an oral discussion on a controversial statement. It also gives students
the chance to practice the use of linking devices in a meaningful situation.

Procedure

1. After a discussion on a controversial statement, list pro and con
   arguments on the board.
2. Divide class into four groups.
3. Assign each group a number from 1 to 4.
4. Tell students from Groups 1 and 2 to write a paragraph each defend-
   ing the statement that you are working with.
5. Tell students from Groups 3 and 4 to write a paragraph each criticiz-
   ing the statement that you are working with.

   Then have Group 1 write the first paragraph
                   Group 2 write the second paragraph
                   Group 3 write the third paragraph
                   Group 4 write the fourth paragraph.

6. All members of the groups must have a copy of their paragraphs.
7. Form four new groups with one member of each of the former ones,
   so that each new group is like this:

St. from Group 1	St. from Group 2
St. from Group 3	St. from Group 4

8. Ask your students to join the paragraphs through the use of linking devices and make the necessary arrangements in their paragraphs so that they acquire the format of an essay.
9. Tell your students to write a fifth conclusive paragraph for the essay.
10. Swap their pieces of writing and have your students compare the different essays produced in the groups.

Contributor

Marcos Cesar Polifemi teaches at the Center for Applied Linguistics, Yazigi, Brazil.

Quotation: Academic Form

Levels
High intermediate +

Aims
Explain, describe, or
persuade

Class Time
30–45 minutes

Resources
One magazine/student
Worksheet (see
Appendix)

This activity shows students how to incorporate another person's ideas into the student's paper.

Procedure

1. Invite the students to find a topic of interest in one of the magazines. Explain that the students will be able to write a report (and/or give a speech on that topic).
2. Pass out the worksheet. Ask students to copy one key sentence from the magazine article onto the worksheet.
3. Write sample introduction sentences like the following on the chalkboard:

   James Smith believes:
   A recent article in *Time* magazine suggests:
   An important idea is discussed by Janet Jones in *People* magazine:

   Have students write a similar but appropriate introduction sentence on their worksheet. (If necessary, explain the use of the colon in this context.)
4. Write sample conclusion sentences like the following on the chalkboard:

   This idea is clearly mistaken.
   Although Smith may be correct, other points of view should be considered.
   Everyone should agree with this opinion.

   Have students write their own sentence on the worksheet.
5. Ask students to fill in the blanks for the footnote section of the worksheet.

6. Ask the students to repeat the activity until they have enough quotes to make a good report. Then combine this activity with other drafting activities: that is, writing an introduction, writing a conclusion.

Caveats and Options

Divide the students into groups of three or four. Ask them to compare one worksheet as a group.

Appendix: Academic Quotations Worksheet

Write the quoted introduction sentence on the line below:

_____

Write the quoted sentence on the line below:

_____

_____

_____ [1]

Write the conclusion sentence on the line below:

_____

Write the name of (1) the author, (2) the title of the article, (3) the title of the magazine, (4) the date of the magazine, (5) the page number in the blanks below.

[1](1) _____ , (2) "_____"

(3) _____ , (4) _____ , p. (5) _____

Contributor

Hugh Rutledge is Head of Faculty at Tokyo International College, Tokyo, Japan.

I'd Like to Ask You a Question

Levels
Advanced

Aims
Report information
gathered graphically

Class Time
1½ hours

Resources
Survey of interest to
learners (e.g., on TV
watching habits,
consumer research)

For academic work, students are required to write project or research papers that entail information gathering. This activity practices devising questionnaires for very simple data gathering and means of reporting the data gathered. This should be a starting point for more sophisticated work required in academic tasks.

Procedure

1. Begin your lesson with an interesting finding, for example, the importance of eating a full breakfast for mental activity and the fact that most people do not do so.
2. Have students contribute possible questions for a questionnaire while you act as secretary writing them on board or transparency. Elicit 10 questions at most.
3. Hold a general discussion on the relevance and format of various questions to devise a questionnaire.
4. Have students answer the questionnaire individually, then gather questionnaires.
5. Discuss with the class and arrive at a consensus on how to collate the questionnaires graphically.
6. Appoint a student to act as secretary and put the incoming information on board.
7. Provide students with the model article, divide the class into small groups, and ask the groups to compare and contrast it with class activity. Have groups report. Point out Subjects, Methodology, Findings. Let each group select a simple topic for a miniresearch paper. Allow complete freedom of topic (e.g., sleeping habits, newspaper purchases). Have each group devise its own questionnaire.

8. For homework: have each student (a) report in writing on the initial class activity, (b) get at least five people to fill out the questionnaire.
9. During the next lesson students share information and work on their reports, making sure the information is represented graphically and in words.
10. Have groups exchange their written reports for questions, queries, clarifications.

Caveats and Options

If you only have one class period do only Steps 1–7, assign homework, and continue next time.

Contributor

Lily Vered is Pedagogical Coordinator as well as a teacher educator and materials developer at the Open University of Israel.

◆ Revision

Helping Students Revise With Process Feedback

Levels
High intermediate

Aims
Develop revising and
editing skills

Class Time
Varies

Resources
List of abbreviations and
short forms used in the
feedback comments in
students' texts

Process feedback is a method of responding to textual and linguistic deficiencies in student writing. Common weaknesses in student essays are lack of substantiation, elliptical writing, egocentric structuring of information, and being too general or too specific at the wrong time. These weaknesses are particularly damaging in essays in which the student has to present and defend a position.

What students need to enable them to revise effectively is guidance on how to think and how to make decisions about meaning selection and language choice. Process feedback gives students such guidance.

Procedure

1. To direct students' thinking, be aware of what they can and cannot do. They generally cannot, for example, correct errors relating to the form and usage of idioms or rectify miscollocation. They can look up the dictionary meaning of a word and see the mismatch between its meaning and their own intended meaning. They can, if they have been taught a reader-centered approach to writing, anticipate their reader's questions and objections.
2. When there are a host of errors and textual flaws in a student's work, select the most serious to give process feedback on. Serious errors are those that result in misunderstanding or a message unsuitable for the situation. It is futile to write feedback comments on every error because there is a limit to how much students can learn at any one time, especially when what has to be learned is not a word list or a set of rules but cognitive strategies springing from a reader-centered/rhetorical-function approach to writing.

3. Consider what the student writer must do to arrive at the desired improvement. Mentally work out the thinking procedures, step by step, leading to a successful revision. For example:

- What is wrong: Failure to elucidate a generally worded idea as in "There should be a more defined dress code in order to eliminate misunderstanding . . . "
- Desired improvement: Writer should make clear what is meant by "more defined."
- Thinking procedures: Recognize that the reader (R) will have a problem understanding "more defined". Identify what detail R needs by predicting R's questions: What do you mean by "more defined"? Defined in what way? Generate ideas for detail. Select the most appropriate.
- Process feedback: Imagine you're the R who has to act on this report. What info must you have to be able to produce a "more defined code"? Jot down R's questions. Think up details. Choose the most helpful for the R.

4. Encourage students to develop self-evaluation capabilities by directing them to look for errors of the same type as one you have pointed out and to use the same feedback comments to guide them in rectifying those errors.

5. After returning the marked essays, allocate time for a conference at which students can ask for help understanding the feedback and rewriting the assignment or a part of it. The feedback comment may include a direction to a student to ask a certain question. If time and resources allow, conferencing should be conducted in small groups or individually.

Appendix: Excerpts from Student Report With Teacher's Process Feedback

Introduction

The implementation of a dress code for students at N University has created misunderstanding[1] between enforcement officers and undergraduates.

As a result, the students' union has requested the Research Services Committee to produce a report on the cause of misunderstanding. This report will give a comprehensive account of the reasons and causes. It will also (facilitate the discussion session)[2] which will be held by the Students Union Council on 21 July 199 . . .

. . . (Methodology and Findings sections follow.)

Discussion . . .

Our [observers noted] that 34% of the students who [wore] bermudas that *are*[3] considered too short are[3] not allowed to enter the library, but 23% who [wore] bermudas that *are*[3] above knee length *are*[3] allowed to enter the library. *This shows that enforcement officers are not uniform in their judgments on the length of bermudas. This further suggest that (different perceptions is the cause of misunderstanding.)[4]

Conclusion

The main cause of misunderstanding[5] over the dress code lies in the lack of specification about what is the acceptable length of bermudas. The authority concerned might have to construct (a more defined dress code)[6] in order to eliminate the misunderstanding.

Teacher's Feedback

[1]Imagine you're a secondary R. Will you get a complete picture of the situation from this paragraph? Ask R's qns about how people know there is misunderstanding. (Note: The terms *secondary reader, primary reader* are repeatedly used in writing lessons in this class.)

[2]Jot down ideas to answer the qn: "What do I want to say?" Think about the relationship bet the report's findings/conclusion and the 21st July session. Look up the word "facilitate" to see if it says what you wish it to mean.

[3]The words in [ ] tell R that you are talking about a past event. But "are" says you are not talking about the past. Think of the effect of the contradiction on the R. find out how to change the verb to say "past".

[4](a)In sentence * you state an interpretation. In this sentence you state the conclusion of an argument that is not there. Think about how * leads to the conclusion.
(b) Predict the R qns. — what R must be told so he/she accepts yr conclusion.
(c) Use these qns to work out the supporting argument to convince R that the cause of misunderstanding is *. Examine the other findings you have. Can any be used to meet R's need for a supporting argument? If you are not sure what a supporting argument is, ask me.

[5]Use (a), (b) and (c) above to evaluate the other parts of your discussion. Have you got supporting arguments to convince R yr interpretation is acceptable?

[6]Imagine you're the R who has to act on this report. What info must you have to be to produce a "more defined code"? Jot down R's qns. Think up details. Choose the most helpful for the R.

Contributor

Antonia Chandrasegaran is an ESL Lecturer at the School of Humanities, Murdoch University, in Perth, Australia.

Revising Checklists for Writing Stories

Levels
Beginning +

Aims
Evaluate a piece of writing
Detect strengths and weaknesses in a story while composing it

Class Time
2–3 hours

Resources
Revising checklist (see Appendix)
Several interesting stories
Copies of several student drafts

When students write a story, they often need help organizing it effectively. The checklist here helps the writer in the process of reading, reflecting, discovering, and improving the draft in order to get the message across clearly and appropriately.

Procedure

1. Select some items from the revising checklist as teaching objectives.
2. Brainstorm with students as to what makes a story effective. For example, having an interesting beginning and ending holds the readers' attention. Note students' ideas on the board.
3. Have students read several interesting stories. Discuss with them how the stories are organized and what makes them effective.
4. Have students form small groups and brainstorm what topics they can write about. Some examples might be dreams, ghost stories, or fictionalized accounts of real events.
5. Invite students to draft their stories in class or at home. Remind students to focus on content and not to worry about accuracy.
6. Tailor the revising checklist by putting the teaching objectives as the items of a revising checklist and adding items students have suggested during previous activities. Select one or two student drafts for discussing the meaning of items on the revising checklist. Duplicate the selected student drafts and the revising checklist as handouts.
7. Distribute the handouts to every student. Explain the items and point of the checklist.
8. Ask small groups of students to share their opinions on the duplicated student drafts for about 5 minutes.
9. Demonstrate how to be a reader and how to give useful feedback.
10. Have small groups peer read drafts and use the checklist to give feedback.
11. Have students rewrite their drafts based on the classmates' feedback.

Caveats and Options

1. Vary the items of your checklist according to your students' abilities and your teaching objectives.
2. Begin with just one or two items for focused revising.

Appendix: Sample Revising Checklist for Writing Stories

Put a tick in the right blank to show your opinion of your classmate's story.

Writer's name: _____   Reader's name: _____

	Yes	No
A. The **title**...		
1. tells me something about the story.	___	___
2. arouses my interest in reading the story.	___	___
B. The **setting**...		
1. tells me where and when the story takes place.	___	___
2. is useful for building up the story.	___	___
3. arouses my interest in reading the story.	___	___
C. The **story**...		
1. has a beginning.	___	___
2. has a middle.	___	___
3. has an end.	___	___
D. When I read the **beginning**,...		
1. I know the setting of the story.	___	___
2. I meet some of the characters.	___	___
3. I learn about the problem or the wish of the characters.	___	___
4. I get interested in the story.	___	___
E. When I read the **middle part**,		
1. I know what happens to the characters in trying to solve the problem or achieve the wish.	___	___
2. I know what happens to the problem or the wish.	___	___
3. I want to keep reading the story to see what will happen next.	___	___
F. When I read the **ending**,...		
1. I get to know how the problem is solved/the wish is achieved.	___	___
2. I find it surprising.	___	___
3. I find it exciting.	___	___
4. I find it hanging in the air.	___	___
5. I find it enjoyable.	___	___
G. I get to know the **characters**...		
1. because of their outlooks.	___	___
2. because of what they say.	___	___
3. because of what they think.	___	___
4. because of what they do.	___	___
H. The **dialogue**...		
1. makes the story easier to read.	___	___
2. makes the story interesting.	___	___
3. tells what the characters are thinking or feeling.	___	___
4. brings out important points.	___	___

Contributor

Marie Cheung is currently pursuing a PhD in TESOL at the City University of Hong Kong.

Cassette Consultations

Levels
Intermediate +

Aims
Revise content and
structure of their written
work

Class Time
Variable

Resources
One audiotape/student
Audiotape recorder with
microphone for teacher
Access to audiotape
players for students

The purpose of this technique is to give students more extensive and useful feedback on their writing than is traditionally given in comments written in the margin, yet without the time constraints of face-to-face conferences. Students also benefit from the listening practice provided by the teacher's comments on the tape.

Procedure

1. Have each student hand in a cassette with each composition.
2. Read each composition and record on the corresponding student's tape your comments on the aspect(s) of writing (e.g., content, organization, mechanics) that you are focusing on.

   a. Try not to address all issues in a single pass. This works especially well for multiple revisions, or process approach, in which organization and content are covered in one draft, mechanics and sentence level grammar in another.
   b. Reference mark the student text before or during recording. Some suggested markings are paragraph numbers, line numbers, or comment numbers (where you place a number near the points of the text that you comment on).
   c. Comments can be as individual as needed but should offer praise as well as points for revision.
   d. Your tone of voice will also communicate a message to the students. A conversational style is appropriate for these tapes.

3. Return tapes and drafts to the students for revision.
4. Students listen to tapes and revise their compositions. Allow time for students to listen to their tapes outside of class and ask questions about anything that was unclear.

112

5. Repeat with subsequent drafts as necessary or desired.

Contributors

Debra Daise and Janis van Zante teach at the University of Colorado, in the United States.

Reading, Revising, Editing

Levels
Intermediate +

Aims
Develop self-evaluation
skills

Class Time
30--40 minutes

Resources
Overhead projector
(OHP)
Transparencies
Markers
200-word composition
by a small group of
students

The idea is to help students develop parameters to evaluate their own texts. The activity is centered on the whole-class revision of a text by a small group of students. It can be repeated until all groups have had a chance to revise.

Procedure

1. Photocopy the text to be revised onto a transparency and also make one normal photocopy of it for each student.
2. Hand out the copies of the composition and ask students to read it. Have a brief class discussion on the general strengths and weaknesses of the text's rhetorical organization, content, and readability.
3. Tell students to put their copies away and display the composition on the OHP. Go over it together and invite them all (including the authors) to make suggestions for improvement. Tell them that you are after not just the correction of grammar and spelling, but that you welcome any change that will enhance the overall quality of the text. Incorporate the suggestions to the text with a nonpermanent marker.

   Note that not all suggestions will be satisfactory: Some may improve grammar but hinder readability; others may be totally unnecessary; others may affect another part of text that will also have to be revised, and so on. It is important that you comment on all suggestions in this way (rather than say only whether the suggestion is good or bad)so that the students can develop a feeling for what it is that they should revise. As you do so, erase the less fortunate revisions and replace them with better ones until you arrive at a satisfactory final draft.
4. Switch off the OHP and ask students to revise their copies of the text on their own for homework.

Contributor

Ana Frankenberg-Garcia teaches English and linguistics in the translation department of a polytechnic in Lisbon, Portugal.

To Write Boldly . . .

Levels
Beginning +

Aims
Revise, edit, rewrite

Class Time
Several sessions

Resources
Writing previously produced

This exercise should encourage greater boldness in rewriting than many inexperienced writers allow themselves. The feedback from peers and from the teacher should emphasize this.

Procedure

1. Distribute writing previously collected so that each student has another student's paper.
2. Tell students to pretend they wrote the papers they have. Have them rewrite the papers, using whatever revising, editing, and rewriting skills are being taught.
3. Collect the finished papers (both versions). It's useful to have both names on the rewritten papers.
4. Without reading the rewritten versions, rewrite all the originals yourself. Again, put your name and the original author's on each of your rewrites.
5. Return all three versions to the first author, and have each one analyze how the three versions differ. Analysis can be free or directed.

Caveats and Options

1. Free comments have ranged from "the rewrite is easier to understand" to notation of spelling changes.
2. A statistical approach can be used with shorter pieces of writing: Have each student count the number of paragraphs, of sentences, and of words in each version and calculate the average words per sentence, sentences per paragraph, etc. This often leads to the insight that both rewriters shortened the original.

Contributor

Ron Grove is Associate Professor in the Department of Area Studies, Mejiro University, Iwatsuki, Japan.

115

Praising Student Writing

Levels
Any

Aims
Develop a positive
attitude toward writing

Class Time
3–15 minutes/draft

Resources
Rough drafts from all
students

Research tells us that many teachers don't write enough positive comments on students' papers. However, when a teacher praises some aspects of a student's writing, the recipient of the praise is likely to develop a positive attitude toward writing, and may then write more on subsequent assignments. Students doing peer editing can be encouraged to open and close their comments with praise of their peers' work. Additional comments, such as questions and suggestions, can be included along with the praise.

Procedure

1. Read the entire paper once only looking for things to praise. Look for what you can praise at the overall text level (the content, the ideas, the thesis) the sentence level, and/or the word level (Daiker, 1989).
2. Use a sentence frame to help you write praise: *I like the way you . . . I like your . . .* (Daiker, 1989).
3. Self-monitor that you have written enough praise by asking yourself if you have written at least three comments of praise on each paper (Daiker, 1989).
4. Remember to keep your students' reading ability in mind when you write the praise especially when writing comments for beginning- and low intermediate-level students. If students have to look up many words from the comments in the dictionary, they may lose interest and not get to enjoy your words of praise.
5. Try to avoid using abbreviations because students have trouble understanding them unless you have specifically taught them.

Caveats and Options

To encourage your students to praise each other's writing, you can give them a handout with a writing sample and a few examples of praise about the content, the sentence level, and the word level of the writing.

References and Further Reading

Daiker, D. (1989). Learning to praise. In C. Anson (Ed.), *Writing and response: Theory, practice, and research* (pp. 103-113). Urbana, IL: National Council of Teachers of English.

Contributor

Ellen Lipp is Associate Professor in the Department of Linguistics at California State University, Fresno, in the United States.

Writing Reader-Friendly Texts

Levels
Intermediate +

Aims
Revise and correct
written work

Class Time
None (work to be done
at home)

Resources
Passages illustrating
points or checklist
Copy of checklist (see
Appendix)

References and Further Reading

Appendix: Checklist for Writing a Reader-Friendly Text

Writing teachers often find themselves concentrating on microcorrections (spelling, grammar, mechanics) to the extent that they overlook the macrolevel, for example, organization, cohesion, and structure. Self-monitoring is preferable because it minimizes the amount of criticism given directly by the teacher. It is important for students to internalize basic guidelines so they can monitor their own writing after completing the course.

Procedure

1. Collect passages illustrating the points you want to cover with your class.
2. Review the principles on the checklist in the Appendix, using the passages you've collected to illustrate the points.
3. Ask each student in the class to use the checklist each time she writes a composition.

Winer, L. (1992). Spinach to chocolate: Changing awareness and attitudes in ESL writing teachers. *TESOL Quarterly, 26,* 57-80.

Before you hand in your work, check the following:

1. Does the title give a good idea of what the text is about?
2. Is there a clearly discernible introduction, body, and conclusion?
3. Does your introduction give your audience a reason for reading the article? For example: While it is commonly thought that women cannot make good soldiers, recent research shows . . . .

4. Does your introduction limit the scope of the discussion? For example: [This article will discuss] three main concepts in human geography.
5. Does each paragraph have a main idea? Are all the sentences in the paragraph about that one idea?
6. Did you talk about what you said you would talk about, for example, three problems of the Middle East, advantages and disadvantages of nuclear power, etc.?
7. Did you clearly state the main idea of the entire text?
8. Did you show the logical connections between paragraphs. For example: *On the other hand*; *The third point is . . .* ?
9. Did you keep in mind who the target audience is? If so, are there any terms that have to be explained? Or did you go into more detail than you had to?
10. Is your conclusion logically related to your introduction? How?
11. Try reading your passage to someone who is similar to the type of audience you had in mind—for example, someone who shares/ doesn't share your cultural background or knowledge about a particular subject. Can he follow your ideas?

Contributor

Beverly A. Lewin teaches in the Division of Foreign Languages, Tel Aviv University, Israel.

Using Prediction to Teach Development

Levels
Advanced

Aims
Develop ideas,
especially during
revision

Class Time
20–30 minutes

Resources
Overhead projector
(OHP)
Transparencies
Student essays

Writing instructors often complain that students fail to develop their ideas sufficiently. Students sometimes do not understand this criticism: They may offer long papers, perhaps loaded with ideas, in their defense. This activity illuminates the problem by isolating instances of underdevelopment and by using an integral part of the reading process—predication—to show how readers' expectations go unfulfilled when writers fail to develop their ideas.

Procedure

1. Select an essay lacking in development (see Appendix for sample).
2. Make a transparency of this essay, then make an overlay that blocks out the text following the idea that the writer fails to develop adequately.
3. Put the transparency on the overhead and have students read up to the blocked out text.
4. Ask students what they think will come next. Usually, they expect further development of the idea. Then show the actual text, which goes on to another, unrelated point without developing the first one. Ask students how they feel about what the writer has done. Usually, they will report being disappointed at the lack of development.
5. Ask the writer—and, if necessary, other students—what more she might say about this point. Usually, the writer will recognize the problem and, alone or with others, generate ideas to solve it.
6. Repeat the sequence as many times as necessary, as in the example.
7. This activity shows the writer—and the entire class—that lack of development is not an arbitrary notion that teachers have about student texts, but a writing problem that her peers have difficulty with.

Appendix: Sample Essay Lacking Development

I think scary movies are O.K. And there are some points I like about those and some point I don't like. [Readers expect the writer to introduce some things he likes, some he dislikes, which he fails to do.]

Things I like about those is that I like being frightened little bit, but not too much. [Readers expect the writer to describe what is "little bit, but not too much," which he fails to do.]

Things I don't like about them is . . .

Contributor

Timothy A. Micek is a doctoral candidate in the Department of English at Illinois State University, in the United States.

Ready, Set, Write

Levels
Advanced

Aims
Develop organizational
and time management
skills

Class Time
1½ hours

Resources
Prepared notes on topic
Essay questions (see
Appendix A)
Criteria for marking (see
Appendix B)
Self assessment sheet
(see Appendix C)

Students prepare detailed notes on a given topic which they can use in mock examination conditions to answer a specific question. They then assess the effectiveness of their preparation and organization of time. They predict their mark by referring to printed criteria.

Procedure

1. Set the theme of the essay several days before the timed piece of work. This enables the students to focus on their revision of the text, make notes and select appropriate quotations. Allow them to cover one sheet of paper with preparatory notes to bring to class with the essay.
2. On the day of the mock examination, give students 45 minutes to consider the question, decide which parts of their notes are relevant to the question set, and make an outline of their essay. You may choose to check these plans briefly before the timed essay begins.
3. At the end of the examination, collect the essays and hand out a self-assessment sheet, plus copies of printed criteria to those who have forgotten to bring their own copy.
4. Have the students fill in the self-assessment sheets.
5. Mark the essay, add feedback, and grade it according to the criteria. Then refer to the self-assessment sheet, adding comments in response to the students' remarks.
6. Meet with each student to discuss the essay and the mark awarded.

Caveats and Options

1. One interesting aspect of working with international students is their perception of the instructor's assessment of written work. For some, it is a mark indicating the value of the written work set against some

unknown criteria; for others it is a sign of personal like or dislike, or a baseline for bargaining.

Self-assessment guides the students toward a realistic understanding of his level of attainment in relation to the task set and the criteria against which it will be marked. It also gives the student an opportunity to write what he would like to say personally to the tutor: "I had trouble with my introduction"; "I didn't check my language thoroughly." "I ran out of time." The admission of a student that he only had time for the first part of the question indicates not only poor time management but a lack of understanding of a necessary balance in the answer.

At the academic level, the most educative section on the self-assessment sheet is the one that asks the student to predict his mark against the criteria. An understanding grows that conventional work ("Everything I know about . . . ") is of low value. Even extensive knowledge of the text is of less value than interpretive skill and flexible manipulation of material in order to answer the question.

2. The decision to show the language mark separately allows you to focus on errors of sentence structure, style, and accuracy without penalizing the student's organization and content.

Appendix A: Sample Timed Essay Questions

West Sussex Institute of Higher Education
Access to BEd (Hons) ESOL
Literature: Drama Assignment
Arthur Miller's *A View from the Bridge*

A timed essay will be set in class on Monday, 15th February at 1:45 p.m. The theme of the essay is conflict.

The title of the timed essay will be given to you in class. You will be allowed 45 minutes to prepare detailed notes and a plan of your essay. The plan should be shown to your tutor, Diana.

After the break you will be allowed approximately 45 minutes to write up your essay.

Your plan and notes should be handed in. They will not receive a mark, but may prove useful as a source of information for feedback.

You will also be asked to fill in a self-assessment sheet before you leave.

Preparation for the Timed Essay

You know that the theme of the title is conflict.

Give time to thinking about conflict in the play. Look at the notes you have made in class and for homework. What kinds of conflict do they cover? Make a list of the kinds of conflict you have noticed. Can you group them? Can you give each group a title or label? Can you trace the cause, the manifestations and the outcome of each type of conflict?

Do not attempt to write an essay.

When you receive the title of the essay you will need to adapt your notes to answer the question set.

West Sussex Institute of Higher Education
Access to BEd (Hons) ESOL
Drama Assignment Monday 15th February, 1993
Arthur Miller: *A View From the Bridge*

With detailed reference to *A View From the Bridge* suggest the cause of the conflict between Eddi and Rudolpho and comment on the consequences for them and for other characters in the play.

You will be allowed approximately 45 minutes to prepare this essay, and 45 minutes to write your preparatory notes in essay form.

The marks for this essay will form 50% of the total marks for this term's drama assignment.

Appendix B: Assessment Criteria Guidelines

Organization and content

Mark

70%-100%

All the qualities of the 60-69% band plus originality, intellectual inventiveness, creative flair or outstanding skill in performance liked with profound interpretive understanding.

60%-69%

Evidence of extensive and thorough study and practice; good capacity to interpret and use material flexibly; notable omissions, errors, irrelevancies or practical inadequacies.

50%-59%

Good grasp of knowledge and practice involved; adequate capacity to manipulate it, but work is conventional with some areas of inadequacy.

40%-49%

Generally adequate level of work but limited interpretative use of knowledge or in some practical skills. Pass.

35%-39%

Limited in range of knowledge and in ability to handle knowledge; limitations in practical skills. Borderline fail.

0%-35%

Insufficient work; irrelevant work; failure to submit. Fail.

Language Level

An additional mark/10 should indicate language level on all major assignments and examinations.

Criteria

9-10

Native fluency in range and complexity. Standards of sentence construction, lexis and grammar are extremely high.

7-8	Near-native fluency in range and complexity. Accurate use of lexis and grammar.
5-6	Sentence construction, lexis and grammar are of an acceptable standard, but minor errors are noticeable.
3-4	Limited range and complexity. Errors in sentence construction, lexis and grammar interfere with reading fluency.
1-2	Severely limited in range of expression. Errors in sentence construction, lexis and grammar interfere with reading fluency.

Appendix C: Sample Self-Assessment Sheet

Self-Assessment: Timed Essay on *A View From the Bridge* (to be filled in on completion of task)

1. Preparation

   Did you find that your preparation during the past week had helped you
   - a. to understand the scope of the title set?
   - b. to organize your notes effectively?

2. Timed preparation in class

   For you, was this
   - a. too much time?
   - b. too little time?

3. Writing the essay

   For you, which was the most difficult aspect
   - a. organizing your answer effectively?
   - b. writing an introduction?
   - c. writing a conclusion?
   - d. using quotations effectively?

4. Look at the criteria for marking in your booklet, then complete this sentence: I believe

I fall into band _____ % because

_____

_____

_____

5. Look at the criteria for awarding a mark for language level. Complete this sentence: I believe I have earned _____ marks because

_____

_____

Signature _____ Date _____

Instructor's comment:

Contributor

Diana Mitchner teaches at the West Sussex Institute of Higher Education, in the United Kingdom.

Peer Response Groups

Levels
Intermediate +

Aims
Revise

Class Time
30–45 minutes in class
(and 30–45 minutes at
home)

Resources
Photocopies of rough
drafts
Peer response sheets

The current popularity of peer response groups is related to a shift in emphasis on written products to an emphasis on process in the teaching of composition. The process approach views prewriting, composing, and revising as overlapping and interconnecting stages. Peer response groups allow students to function as audience and respond to other students' writing, thus enabling students to use each others' comments while revising their drafts. In using peer response groups, it is important to remember that one's writing is an extension of oneself. Students should not be overly critical of other students' writing. It is the responsibility of the teacher to structure peer response groups so that students know exactly what they are expected to do and to create a positive environment in which students encourage each other.

Procedure

1. Explain the rationale for using peer response groups: that is, for students to read and respond to each others' writing so that students can see their writing through the eyes of the readers and can use the readers' comments to revise their drafts.
2. Discuss guidelines explaining how students are expected to interact with each other. These guidelines can include the following:

For the reader:

- Read the drafts carefully (be a good reader)
- Re-read the drafts, fill out peer response sheets, and write down your reactions as you read
- In class, while discussing each others' drafts, don't quarrel with other readers' reactions
- Be prepared—your group depends on you to contribute.

For the writer:

- If you want comments about a particular part of your draft, ask
- Be attentive and listen carefully to the readers' comments
- Don't argue, reject, or justify
- Remember that comments from your group members are suggestions and that it's your draft—you make the final decisions about how to write it.

3. Arrange or let students arrange themselves in groups of two, three, or four.
4. Ask students to bring in and exchange photocopies of their drafts (one copy for each group member and one for the teacher).
5. Distribute peer response sheets (teacher-generated questions to which students respond). The content of the questions varies according to the level of the class and the purpose of the writing assignment. Sample questions include:

- What do you think is the focus of this draft?
- What evidence does the writer give to support the focus?
- What do you like best about this draft?
- What does this draft mean to you? What did you get out of it?

6. Using a former student's first draft, work through the peer response sheet together as a class to help students understand how to respond.
7. Ask students to respond in writing to each others' drafts and to complete the peer response sheets either in class or at home.
8. Ask students to meet in their groups to discuss each others' drafts, elaborating on their written comments. It seems to work best if, for example, Students A, B, and C all discuss D's draft before switching to C's draft.
9. Explain that when students finish discussing all the drafts, they should return the peer response sheets and the photocopies with written comments on them to the writers.
10. Return your photocopies with comments on them to the writers.
11. Ask students to use these oral and written responses from students and teacher to rewrite their drafts.

Caveats and Options

1. An important and complex issue related to peer response groups is the correction of grammar errors. ESL students frequently miscorrect other students' grammar; therefore, it makes sense that they should be discouraged from correcting grammar. You can do it.
2. Peer response groups also provide a forum for speaking English in an authentic communicative situation.
3. An unsupportive social climate in peer response groups can lead to defensiveness and withdrawal (Gere, 1987). It is absolutely essential that students not be overly critical of each others' drafts and learn to praise the writing of other students.

References and Further Reading

Elbow, P. (1973). *Writing without teachers*. New York: Oxford University Press.

Gere, A. R. (1987). *Writing groups: History, theory, and implications*. Carbondale, IL: Southern University Press.

Contributor

Gayle Nelson is Assistant Professor in the Department of Applied Linguistics, Georgia State University, in the United States.

Giving and Getting Feedback

Levels
Intermediate +

Aims
Revise a piece of
writing
Share writing with
others

Class Time
1+ hours

Resources
Draft of essay
Copy of response guide
(see Appendix)

This activity helps students become more critical readers of their own writing. It also helps them become more confident in supporting the choices they've made in their drafts and gives them an additional source of feedback on their writing.

Procedure

1. After students have finished a draft, divide them into pairs and have them read each other's paper. (This step could be done as homework).
2. Give students a copy of the response guide.
3. Have students answer the questions on the guide.
4. Have students talk about their responses with their partner. (They should discuss their answers after each question, but they can wait until they have finished answering all the questions.)
5. Each team of students meets with the teacher to discuss the comments on the response guides, asking the students to explain their choices. The teacher then gives some suggestions.
6. Students then make any desired changes in their draft.

Appendix: Response Guide

Writer _____

Editor _____

Give specific answers to the questions below. Answer each question completely. If a question has more than one part, answer every part. General yes/no answers will not be much help to the writer.

1. Carefully read the introduction. What is the writer's main idea? Has the writer captured the attention of the reader? How did he do it? According to the introduction, what topics will be covered in the

paper? In what order will they be presented? Finally, has the writer left out any information that needs to be included in the introduction? What suggestions can you make?

2. Look at the body of the essay. Does each paragraph contain a main idea statement? List those that do not.

3. Is the information presented in a logical manner? What changes would you suggest?

4. Look at the conclusion? What is its purpose? Is it effective? Can you suggest a different type?

5. Look at the transactions from the introduction to the body and the body to the conclusion. Do they seem logical? Can you suggest any improvements?

6. Look at the transitions between paragraphs in the body. Do they make sense? (Are they easy to follow?) If not, list them below. How can they be changed?

7. Look at the vocabulary in the paper. If there are words that are unfamiliar to you, circle them on the draft and discuss them.

8. Does the paper contain a variety of sentence structures? If not, can you suggest some changes that could be made?

9. What are the areas of the paper that need the most improvement?

10. What are the strengths of the paper?

Contributor

Michael O'Bryan teaches at the American Language Institute, Indiana University of Pennsylvania, in the United States.

Peerless Peer Review

Levels
Advanced

Aims
Revision

Class Time
50–90 minutes

Resources
Guidelines in the form
of a worksheet (see
Appendix)

The purpose of peer review as a tool for revision is to further the student ability to internalize guidelines for writing and to give them suggestions for improving their essays and reactions to the essay from their peers. Peer review can also help students internalize guidelines.

Procedure

1. Prepare a worksheet with questions pertaining to the essay being written with ample room below each question for the student to answer it. Prepare two copies for each student. Don't write any questions that can be answered with yes or no only.
2. On the day that the rough draft of the essay is due, collect all typewritten, double-spaced essays at the beginning of class.
3. Put students into heterogeneous groups of three to five students and distribute worksheets to everyone.
4. Distribute the essays you just collected, one to each student. Do not give any group an essay that belongs to someone in that group.
5. Instruct students that this essay is a rough draft and will not be graded; therefore, it is going to be helpful for everyone if the questions on the worksheet are answered honestly and constructively. Constructive, honest answers will help the student whose paper is being critiqued to improve her paper. Instruct them also that their critique will be handed in with the final draft of the essay. This seems to make students feel accountable (You can grade the critique sheet at that time if you want to).
6. At the end of class they give the critique sheet(s) back to the writer and rough draft or final version to you (if you are collecting rough drafts for teacher feedback—if not, the writer would get the essay

133

back along with the critique sheet(s) to begin revising, using her peers' suggestions and reactions.

Appendix: Sample Worksheet

1. What style does the writer use to introduce the paper?
2. What is the thesis statement?
3. Where is the thesis located? Does the thesis state the position of the writer?
4. What is the writer arguing for or against?
5. What support (reasons) does the writer give for the thesis? Name three reasons the writer gives to support the thesis.

   a.
   b.
   c.

6. Does the writer use examples or quotations to support the thesis? Name three examples or quotations the writer uses.

   a.
   b.
   c.

7. How does the writer conclude the essay?
8. Did the writer convince you of her or his position? How?
9. Name three things you liked about this essay.
10. Give three suggestions for improving the essay.

Contributor

Jean Bernard Porter teaches ESL at the Center for English as a Second Language at the University of Arizona.

Working Toward Self-Sufficiency

Levels
Low intermediate; adults

Aims
Edit and revise written work

Class Time
30–40 minutes

Resources
Self- and peer-revision sheets (see Appendix)

Research shows that peer revision (a) saves the teacher time, (b) helps students become independent learners, (c) forces students to apply their knowledge about writing, (d) requires students to use all language skills while they negotiate disagreements and misunderstandings about content, discourse features and grammar.

Experienced teachers report that students perform peer revision better when criteria are detailed and specific. Open-ended questions such as, "Is everything correct?" overwhelm and frustrate students. On the other hand, specific questions about content (e.g., Did you include two specific points to support your argument? Write one of the points here.) and grammar (e.g., Go back and check all the verbs. Are they in the correct form and tense?) will help students focus on relevant material.

As students practice revision, they gain confidence in themselves and the writing process and learn to check their peers' and their own work automatically. They become self-sufficient, which is essential for their academic and vocational success.

Procedure

1. Before students begin writing their compositions, tell them other people in the class will be reading their papers. Emphasize how important handwriting legibility is.
2. After students have written their compositions, give them each a self-revision form. If the class has never done this activity before, put the form on an overhead projector and do it together as a class. Encourage students to correct their errors as they go down the list of questions on the form. Explain that this technique is a way for them to write better by critically looking at their own writing.
3. After students have completed their self-revision forms, put students in pairs and give each student a peer-evaluation form. Ask students

to exchange papers and read their partner's paper, answering the questions on the form. Instruct the students to stop and ask their partner anytime they are confused about any part of the composition. The point is to engage the students in conversation about meaning before they isolate grammar errors. You should be walking around the room helping students revise.

4. When students have finished doing the peer-evaluation forms, encourage them to rewrite their draft making the necessary revisions and then turn it in. Only after the paper has gone through a self- and peer-revision do you grade the composition. Students then must reflect on your comments and respond to them.

References and Further Reading

Keh, C. L. (1990). Feedback in the writing process: A model and methods for implementation. *ELT Journal, 44,* 294-304.

Leki, I., & Silva, T. (Eds.). (1992). *Journal of Second Language Writing, 1.*

Reid, J. (1993). *Teaching ESL writing.* Englewood Cliffs, NJ: Prentice Hall Regents.

Appendix: Revision Forms for an Argumentation/ Persuasion Composition

Peer-Revision

My name is _____ and I am evaluating _____ paper.

Circle the correct answer.
1. Is anything you read confusing to you?
    yes   no
If the answer is yes, talk to your partner and fix the confusing parts.
2. Did your partner give three reasons to support his or her opinion?
    yes   no
Write one of the reasons of support here.
4. Did your partner use transitions to connect the ideas?
    yes   no   sometimes
What are some of the transitions he or she used?
5. Are all the verbs in the correct tense and form? (Go back and look.)
    yes   no   sometimes
6. Are all the words spelled correctly?
    yes   no   sometimes
7. Did you have any trouble reading your partner's handwriting?
    yes   no   sometimes
8. Did every sentence begin with a capital letter?
    yes   no   sometimes
9. Did every sentence end with a period?
    yes   no   sometimes
10. Did you enjoy reading this composition?
    yes   no   sometimes

Why or why not?

Teacher's comments:

Student's comments to teacher:

I think my strengths in writing this paper are:

I think my weaknesses in writing this paper are:

The next time I do a writing assignment, I will try not to make the same mistakes (sign your name) _____

Self-Revision

Name:

Circle the correct answer.
1. Does your topic sentence give your opinion?
   yes   no
2. Do you have three reasons to support your opinion?
   yes   no
3. Do you have transitions that connect your reasons?
   yes   no   sometimes
4. Are you sure that another student can read your paper?
   yes   no   sometimes
5. Go back and check all the verbs in your paragraph. Are all the verbs in the correct form and tense?
   yes   no   sometimes
6. Did you start every sentence with a capital letter?
   yes   no   sometimes
7. Did you end every sentence with a period?
   yes   no   sometimes
8. Did you indent your paragraphs?
   yes   no   sometimes
9. Are you sure that all the words are spelled correctly?
   yes   no   sometimes
10. Was it difficult for you to write this composition?
    yes   no   sometimes
    If the answer is yes, why was it difficult?

Contributors

Donna Price-Machado teaches ESL to adults for the San Diego Community College District. Ingrid Greenberg trains teachers and is a consultant in Texas for Harcourt Brace, ESL.

Correction Symbols: Developing Editing Skills

Levels
Any

Aims
Proofread and edit

Class Time
30 + minutes

Resources
Correction symbols
handout
Students' written work

Many writing teachers spend a great deal of time correcting errors that their students could correct themselves with proper proofreading. Teachers can implement a system of feedback early in a writing course, through the use of correction symbols to help students become aware of the types of errors they make. After repeated experiences correcting these errors—identified by the teacher—students incorporate the identification and correction of similar errors into their proofreading and editing. Over time, students integrate proofreading into their writing habits without teacher intervention. The result is more accurate, responsible work on the part of students, allowing the teacher to focus on aspects of students' writing that students are less able to improve on their own during proofreading and subsequent revision.

Procedure

1. Devise a set of correction symbols that you feel comfortable with and create a handout that lists them all. See the example below:

Correction Symbols: Use Them to Improve Your Writing

⊂	capitalization problem
⬡	incorrect word order (correct word but misplaced)
∧	missing word(s)
P	punctuation
—	correct word family, but incorrect word form
SP	spelling problem
art	incorrect article (a/an/the/Ø)
ww	wrong word choice
(,	incomplete sentence (fragment)
¶	indentation needed
⌣	words need to be combined
(R)	run-on sentence
✕	unnecessary
(?)	I don't understand. Try again.

---

2. Collect writing samples from all students early in a writing course. Provide feedback on the writing samples by using your set of correction symbols to identify errors that you think your students can correct on their own.

3. Create a training session worksheet that will introduce students to the set of correction symbols that will be used throughout the course. Select faulty sentences from students' own written work that allow you to incorporate as many correction symbols as possible onto the worksheet; try to include at least one sentence from each of your students on the worksheet. Using students' own sentences is a useful tactic because students will be able to identify their own sentences and will realize that these are real mistakes rather than textbook mistakes. Worksheet entries might look like these examples:

> a. The best day in my life _is_ my wedding day **P**
>
> b. What an estrange custom americans have. *art sp c*
>
> c. Americans eat often canned foods and fast foods.
>
> d. The Queen Elizabeth II has movies to children. *ww*

4. Introduce students to the use of correction symbols for writing improvement. First, distribute the handout with all the correction symbols and remind students that they will refer to it throughout the school year. Go over the symbols, one at a time, with example sentences on the chalkboard. Use straightforward, simple examples so that students can focus on the symbol and its uses rather than be distracted by complicated vocabulary and complex language structures. For example, to introduce the symbol for incorrect word order, you might use a simple example like the one below:

It's a building large

To introduce the symbol for correct word family but incorrect word form, you might want to provide students with numerous examples:

He spoke *quick*.
She *go* to the library to do her homework yesterday.
The people are fighting for their *free*.

Once students have been introduced to all the symbols, distribute the training session worksheet and have students work on it individually. Circulate around the classroom and provide necessary assistance so that students can correct the faulty sentences while making use of the symbols.

5. Return work that has been edited with correction symbols. Have them edit their work, using the symbols to guide their decisions. These rewrites can be done in class or at home.
6. Collect students' edited written work and evaluate their effectiveness in using the symbols to improve their writing.
7. Throughout the course, use these correction symbols to help students learn to identify their most common nonnegotiable errors during editing stages in the writing process. Later in the course, after students begin to see patterns in their written work, encourage them to look for their most frequent errors when proofreading their work on their own.

Contributor

Fredricka L. Stoller teaches at Northern Arizona University, in the United States.

Using Outlines to Revise

Levels
Advanced

Aims
Explain or persuade

Class Time
45–50 minutes

Resources
Copies of a sample expository or persuasive essay
Complete draft of an expository or persuasive essay

In the process of composing an expository or persuasive essay, ESL students often have difficulty shaping their ideas and materials into a coherent, logical pattern and also in detecting structural deficiencies while revising. These two areas of difficulty can be best addressed when students, having completed a draft, help each other in peer response groups.

Procedure

If the students have learned how to make a formal outline in complete sentences, start with Step 2; if they haven't, start with Step 1.

1. Hand out copies of a sample essay by a student from another class and demonstrate how to make a formal outline for it.
2. Organize the students into groups of three or four, taking care to mix students of different writing proficiency levels and different nationalities.
3. Have the students pass their draft to their right, read it, and write a formal outline. When the outlining is done, they should pass this draft on but keep the outline. Repeat this step until every student gets his or her own draft back.
4. Have the students make an outline for their own draft. At this point, when they have read two or three other students' drafts and made outlines for them, they are enriched by the ideas and organizational possibilities presented in those other students' drafts. So they may more readily see the weaknesses in their own draft. In making an outline for it, they have an opportunity to see what has been accomplished in the draft and what could be done to give it a more coherent and logical structure.
5. Now let the students have the outlines the other students have made for their draft. They should compare all these outlines with their own, and with their draft. They'll be happy seeing their expository or

persuasive aims recognized by their peers. But they have to think hard when they find differences between their own perceptions of the draft and their peers'. They may feel that some of their peers have misunderstood them. They should be encouraged to discuss with their peers what they think is misconstrued. Very often those are instances of writer's intentions unfulfilled: What the writer intended to say doesn't quite come through. While studying the outlines and discussing them, student writers can find areas for improvement through independent, active thinking rather than passive acceptance of an authority's instructions.

6. Ask the students to write down their thoughts about how to revise the draft. When this is done, have students revise the draft at home with particular attention to improving its overall structure.

Contributor

George Q. Xu teaches in the Department of English, Clarion University, in the United States.

◆ Examination Writing

Writing Under Examination Conditions

Levels
Intermediate +

Aims
Interact successfully
with an exam topic to
produce an acceptable
product

Class Time
30–45 minutes

Resources
Appropriate exam topics
(see Appendix)
Overhead projector
(OHP)

In an exam situation, writers are left on their own, with only the title as a prop. Following the development of process writing skills, they need training in the process of interacting with a title in order to be able to produce a product acceptable to the examiners. They will not be able to draft and redraft their work and will have to work to a tight schedule. They need, however to adopt a controlled, organized approach to the task, rather than setting off at breakneck speed. They also need to allow themselves some time to proofread their work.

Procedure

1. Write an exam title (of the type students will face) on the board, or project it on an OHP. Ask students to work together in pairs or small groups on the following framework:

   - What am I being asked to do? How many parts are there to the question?
   - Which language structures/functions do I need to include?—for example, past tenses for past narratives, functions for giving advice etc.
   - What fictitious elements do I have to invent?
   - Which vocabulary items from my current lexicon might I include?
   - Who is the covert addressee? That is, what is the appropriate register?
   - What formal features do I need to include? For example, addresses for letters, paragraphs

- What criteria are being used to assess me? For example, accuracy/ fluency, communicative ability, length (you should provide this information).

2. Give feedback and then have students write the task together, either partly or wholly in class. Finished products can be put up on the wall for general reading and discussion. With the right atmosphere, students can even assess each other's work according to the exam guidelines (some exam boards publish past compositions with grades awarded; these are useful in setting standards).

3. As students become familiar with the activity, they can start working on their own, with a time limit—around 10% of the exam time available can be spent on this frameworking stage. A similar proportion of time should be spent proofreading.

4. Finally, mock exam questions can be tackled with the whole process of frameworking, writing and proofreading being done in class.

Appendix: Sample Framework

Title: You have recently discovered the address of a friend whom you haven't seen for 5 years. Write a letter telling him/her about the changes in your life and suggesting a meeting.

See Step 1 in Procedure

1. Informal letter: describing changes, suggesting
   Introduction: Greeting, reason for writing
   2nd Paragraph: My news—changes. Ask about his news?
   3rd Paragraph: Suggest meeting. Close letter.
2. Present Perfect (recently) + Continuous "... *been doing.*" Past Simple (date).
   Suggestions: *"What about ... ing?" "Why don't we ... "*
   Invitations: *"Would you like to ... ?"*
   Opening/Closing: *"Dear ... /Looking forward to hearing from you ... Best wishes."*
3. The friend: a friend from university. Changes: started new job in bank, moved to a new flat. The meeting: dinner at my new flat.
4. *came across* your address, *get in touch, exciting* job, *cozy* flat.
5. Friend—informal—*"Hi!" "How're things"* ...

6. Only my address. Three paragraphs.
7. Communicate message with awareness of audience and reasonable degree of accuracy, for example, errors do not interfere with meaning. (Depends on the criteria of the exam board).

Contributor

Kenneth Dean is Examinations Officer at the Cultura Inglesa, Sao Paulo, Brazil.

Writing Answers to Essay Questions

Levels
Intermediate +

Aims
Write acceptable
answers to essay
questions

Class Time
20–30 minutes

Resources
Colored markers

Knowing how to write answers to essay questions can be a culturally specific skill. In Western academia, this is one of the most common ways to show one's mastery of material. To be successful, students need to understand what constitutes well and poorly written essay answers.

Procedure

1. Have students write essay answers to questions about a reading passage and hand them in.
2. To mark their answers, use a set of colored markers and a color-coded system to highlight the strong and weak points of each student's work. Each color signifies something different, for example:

   green = good point, good paraphrase, important detail, good summary
   yellow = paraphrase problem
   blue = superfluous information
   pink = not clearly expressed, not natural English

3. Before returning the students' work the next day, write on the board the names of students who had well-written answers to the respective essay questions.
4. After returning their work, encourage students to read each others' answers (particularly those listed on the board as having been good ones) and to compare the strong and weak points of their own with those of others.

Caveats and Options

By referring to the colored markings on their papers, students can focus on the strengths and weaknesses of their own and others' answers in a manner that is visually and conceptually clear to students, as well as efficient for both teacher and students.

Even without the color-coded system, asking students to share and compare their work can be of value, especially for students who have not done well on an assignment. However, with the coded highlighting, they can more readily identify what to focus on. Perhaps the greatest benefit is that, having been spared the teacher's lecture on the shortcomings of their own answers, they have the opportunity to analyze for themselves the quality of their own and others' work. This can culminate in an opportunity to enhance their awareness and their own analytical skills of good versus poor answers. A heightening of both their awareness and their analytical capabilities should provide them with a firmer base for their next attempt at writing essay answers.

Contributors

David and Peggy Kehe teach at the Minnesota State University-Akita, in Japan.

◆ Portfolios

Portfolios: Curricular Design and Assessment

Levels
Any

Aims
Understand a variety of
writing genres
Reflect upon own
writing processes

Class Time
Over time: during a
school year, a semester,
or entire enrollment in
an institution

Resources
Notebook with dividers

What are portfolios? They are collections, representing students' writing or their interaction with an academic or cultural context. The entries in portfolios are selected as representative of the goals of the class or program curriculum. In most classes, the teacher selects some entries; the students select others. Entries are collected over time so that students and faculty can assess their own growth and change. Each entry in the portfolio requires a written reflection, on the part of the students, thus enhancing the development of metacognitive awareness of their writing processes. In most situations, portfolio entries are graded before they are entered into the portfolio. The entire portfolio, with its four or five entries, reflections upon the entries and the introduction to the reader, can be scored, through discussion and consensus, by teacher and curriculum designers.

Procedure

1. First, and foremost, make decisions about the goals for the students and the writing program. These will determine portfolio entries and assessment measures.
2. Then, make decisions about the part that the portfolios will play in the students' placement or final assessment. Will the assessment of portfolios at the end of the term be the principal tool? Will portfolios represent X% of the final grade?
3. Make decisions about portfolio entries. How many will there be? What types of writing will be selected for the portfolio entries?
4. Make decisions about when and how the entries will be evaluated. For example, will each paper that is included in the portfolio be graded when it is originally turned in to the teacher? (Reflections are not graded, for the most part.)

5. Make decisions about the nature of the reflections based upon each entry. For example, if the students are permitted to select a "wild card" (i.e., any writing of their choice), they might be asked to answer the following questions in their reflection: Why did you choose this piece of writing? Why is it important to you? What does it tell us about you as a reader or writer? Are there other writings that you also considered including?

6. Make decisions about the introduction to the portfolio. When will it be written? What form will it take?

7. Finally there are decisions about evaluation. Will portfolios be evaluated by a single teacher? Should group evaluation take place? If so, how should portfolios be scored?

Contributor

Ann M. Johns teaches in the Department of Rhetoric and Writing Studies, San Diego State University, in the United States.

Using the Portfolio Approach

Levels
Low intermediate +

Aims
Revise and refine texts

Class Time
Varies

Resources
Paper
Self-evaluation sheets

In developing a finished portfolio, students learn how to use the process approach and develop confidence in their ability to improve their writing. The portfolio method allows you to teach students individually how to revise and to evaluate their own work. The finished portfolio can be evaluated for a variety of purposes—student evaluation, program evaluation, developing a work-sample portfolio, and establishing reference materials for the student.

Procedure

For Business Documents

1. After initial discussion and problem-solving activities for each exercise, have students write each document and submit it for evaluation.
2. As a self-evaluation tool, ask students to complete a checklist appropriate for the particular document. A checklist for a routine request might include these questions:

   - Is the message direct—does it begin with a request for information or assistance?
   - Is the document format appropriate for the type of message?
   - Are the items enumerated in a vertical listing?

3. Evaluate and/or discuss the document with the student.
4. Have the student revise the document as often as necessary with conferences scheduled appropriately (for a long or complicated document, more than one discussion may be necessary).
5. Ask students to prepare a semipermanent folder with an appropriate title page so that the finished portfolio can be graded as a whole and can then be used by the student (possibly with one last revising session) as a sample of communication skills during a job interview,

and also as a desk reference. To be the most useful, the portfolio should contain a variety of types of documents.

6. To determine grades, assign a total number of points for the entire portfolio, determine the number of points per page, and deduct half the points for a page that is not usable.

For Course or Program Evaluation

1. Have students prepare a rough draft for each of the pieces to be included (a good portfolio might include four pieces—perhaps a piece of personal writing, a research project, an argumentative essay, and a summary/analysis from a content class.)
2. Throughout the process of writing each assignment, schedule conferences to discuss purpose, ideas, form, organization, and structure with the student. In this way, you can serve as coach and educator rather than as judge or task master.
3. Have the student revise each document until it represents the student's ability.
4. Allow the student to select the pieces to be included in the portfolio.
5. Evaluate the portfolio appropriately for your purpose. For example, a pass/fail grade could be assigned if the purpose was simply to determine the competency of a student to handle the work at the next level; a point system could be used if class standings or grades needed to be determined.

Contributor

Esther J. Winter teaches in the Department of English, Northwest Missouri State University, in the United States. Janet Winter is Associate Professor in the Department of Management at Central Missouri State University, in the United States.

Part III: Expressive Writing

Editor's Notes

Expressive—or creative—writing tends to be writer rather than reader centered, and within an expressive view of writing, such characteristics as integrity, spontaneity, sincerity, and originality are valued, although as Faigley (1986) points out, these are difficult to assess. Peter Elbow, in his (1973) *Writing Without Teachers,* promoted organic spontaneity, and his approach has been very influential, particularly in the teaching of writing in the native English classroom. Although expressive writing risks becoming self-centered, which is the antithesis of the type of reader-focused writing discussed in the introduction to Part II, Academic Writing, the kind of organic development associated with expressive writing does have a useful role within an eclectic approach to the teaching of writing.

Indeed, for some students, an opportunity to exercise imagination and self-expression may prove highly motivating. Expressive writing does not, of course, have to aim at literary goals. Imaginative and creative writing can be promoted at quite elementary levels, drawing on such universal genres as the story, the fable, and the fairy tale. These genres embody fundamental elements such as a narrative sequence, a plot, conflict and resolution, as well as a moral (or point), without which any writing, expressive or otherwise, lacks focus and purpose. By developing an awareness of such elements within the context of imaginative writing, learners will have acquired concepts that can be transferred to other types of writing.

Another pay off from expressive writing concerns intercultural sharing when working with nationally mixed groups of students. Fables and tales, in particular, illustrate and embody significant values, the sharing of which through story telling can encourage intercultural understanding. Finally, stories are the most fundamental literary form, and through varied techniques for devising, telling, and sharing stories, learners will engage in group activities that shift expressive writing from the egocentric to the social.

References

Faigley, L. (1986). Competing theories of process: a critique and a proposal. *College English, 86,* 527-542.

Elbow, P. (1973). *Writing without teachers.* New York: Oxford University Press.

◆ Stories and Narratives
Composing a Narrative

Levels
Beginning

Aims
Compose a narrative
piece to report past
actions

Class Time
1½ hours

Resources
Set of detailed pictures
or drawings showing a
progressive action
without an ending

This activity asks beginning-level students to use known structure and vocabulary to describe a series of events. This will provide the basis for narrating a real sequence of events after observation.

Procedure

1. Review the difference between the simple present and present continuous with students.
2. Give each student a series of pictures showing a related sequence of events. Ask students to identify known and unknown vocabulary in each picture as one student records vocabulary for each picture on the board.
3. Ask students to write one sentence about each picture in the sequence. Tell them to leave four to five lines blank after each of their sentences.
4. When students have finished, ask them to exchange papers with another student, read the sentences their partner has written, and help their partner to correct any mistakes in grammar, syntax or spelling.
5. Ask students to keep their papers and write an additional sentence for each picture in the sequence, under the original author's sentence. Explain to the students that this sentence is to provide more detail and description or to depict another action happening in the picture.
6. When students have finished, ask them to take the new sentences they have written and repeat Steps 4 and 5 with a new partner.
7. This process is best repeated three times. However, if the pictures are particularly rich in detail, continue until you notice students begin having trouble thinking about what to write. (Students usually

have an easy time writing details or actions that their partners have "missed," so if it is getting difficult for them, move on to Step 8.)

8. After the final sentence corrections are made, ask students to return their papers to the author of the first sentence. The original author can now edit her short story by rearranging the sentences as she likes. Ask students to write a draft of the entire story and read it to a partner of their choice. The partners can now suggest further alterations focusing on clarity and organization.

9. Ask students to complete the story with an unexpected or surprise ending. This activity can be a good homework assignment or, if it is done in class, it can give the teacher an opportunity to work with individual students needing assistance.

10. Give 10 minutes of class time for students to check the ending of their story with other students for corrections and editing suggestions. Ask students to write the final draft at home.

11. A nice way to end this activity is to ask for volunteers to read the story aloud. Students rarely feel anxious about presenting this work to the class as it has been a joint effort. Put all stories on public display for class members to read during breaks.

Contributor

Elizabeth Bodnar teaches at the South Gate Middle School in Los Angeles, California, in the United States.

Discourse Dictoglosses

Levels
High intermediate +

Aims
Narrate a story

Class Time
2 hours

Resources
Sample discourse
dictogloss (see
Appendix)

Procedure

1. Choose key cohesive devices (e.g., *the other day, eventually, finally, even when*) from a text (see Appendix).
2. Ask students, individually, to write accurate sentences containing those phrases.
3. As students report back, put sentences on the board, eliciting different word order possibilities, and eliciting key concepts too.
4. Elicit key lexis (e.g., *to choose, to leap, to bounce, to sob*).
5. Tell students you're going to tell them a story with the grammar/lexical items practiced. Ask them to guess the story.
6. Tell students you're going to read the story three times, each time at normal speed. Draw an imaginary sheet of paper on the board and indicate that they should only write in the center of the page and that they should write on every third line. Tell students they should only write key words and not attempt to write whole sentences.
7. Read the story out for the first time. Then ask some students how many words they were able to get down.
8. Read aloud the story two more times. Tell students beforehand that they should try to fit the new words in the right places on their sheets.
9. Split the class into groups of approximately four, making sure each group has both linguistically weaker and stronger students. Tell the class that each group must try to reconstruct the story with the words they have. It's important that each student write down the agreed group story.
10. Get students to regroup, so that each new group contains members of the previous groups. Ask students in each new group to compare scripts and to make changes, if they wish.

11. Elicit the story from the class. Tell them if the sentences they produce are grammatically correct or not (i.e., don't say whether they have exactly the same sentences as in the original text).
12. Distribute photocopies of the original text. Have students check their versions against the original.
13. Ask students in pairs to exchange memorable experiences they have had—whether positive or negative.
14. Ask if any students would like to tell the whole class about their experience.
15. Ask students to write a story entitled "A Memorable Experience" (either in class or for homework).

Appendix: Sample Dictogloss

The other day I was in Ramsgate chasing my kids on the rocks on the cliff top just outside King George the Sixth's Park. I must have tried to leap from one rock to another because I remember missing my landing and turning over in mid air. Eventually my back hit a clump of rocks, and I bounced off these, and finally fell down onto the ground below. When I was in mid air, time seemed to stand still. I remember thinking that I might die or be crippled for life. Even when I got up from the fall, I couldn't believe what had happened to me. I started sobbing uncontrollably and tried to make my way back to the car.

Contributor

Paul Bress teaches in the English Studies Centre at Hilderstone College, in England.

Piranha

Levels
Intermediate

Aims
Describe imaginary or
real experience

Class Time
30–40 minutes

Resources
Handout (see
Appendix)

This activity helps learners build up an extended text by way of controlled, guided, and freer episodes in the writing process.

Procedure

1. Ask the students what they know about piranhas.
2. Have pairs of students try to complete the first paragraph of a handout (see Appendix on next page). Check their work as a class.
3. Repeat with subsequent paragraphs.
4. The students then expand the two paragraphs, on their own or in pairs.
5. Have the students complete the exercise on their own. (Obviously the students could do the whole exercise on their own.)

Continued

Appendix: Handout

Piranha!

Piranhas are _____ fish found _____. They have
developed a _____ method _____ their prey. They have great
appetites for _____ and _____. They travel in
_____ and _____ to skeletons in a matter of
_____. They look like _____. They have
_____ bodies, _____ heads, and their jaws are
_____ with _____ teeth.

Rearrange the following sentences and expand them into two paragraphs.

1. We were there on an expedition to study the wildlife.

2. We did not manage much sleep and were up before sunrise.

3. We set off up the swelling river as the dawn broke and the birds woke the
   rest of the forest with their screeching.

4. Once I had a terrifying experience with piranhas.

5. We stayed in a dreadful hotel with only a single fan battling against the
   sticky heat in the bedroom.

6. I went with my family to Manaus, way up the Amazon in the thick
   tropical forests.

Contributor

*Anthony Bruton teaches in the Faculty of Philology, University of
Seville, Spain.*

Building a Story

Levels
Beginning +

Aims
Write a descriptive short story

Class Time
30 minutes–1 hour

Resources
List of vocabulary words
The first sentence of a story

This activity gives students practice using new vocabulary in context, while at the same time allowing them an opportunity to compose original sentences. It also gives the teacher some quality one-on-one time with the students. This activity can be used with any size class.

Procedure

The following instructions assume that learners are sitting in a circle.
1. Write the first sentence of a story on the board. For example:

   One day _____ was walking down the street when he/she saw a wallet on the sidewalk. He/she picked it up, opened it, and found it contained $10,000!

   Ask the students to copy this onto a piece of paper, inserting their own name in the blank, and choosing the appropriate pronouns.

2. After everyone has copied the sentence, ask them to pass their paper to the person on their right.
3. Write your first vocabulary word on the board. Explain to the students they must now write a second sentence on their neighbor's paper that:

   - uses the vocabulary word you have written on the board
   - follows the first sentence in meaning
   - contains an action verb (e.g., *run, eat, swim, sleep, go.* Words such as *feel, hope, want,* are not action verbs. This rule helps ensure a more interesting story.)

4. While the students are writing the second sentence, walk around the room offering suggestions or making corrections. It may take anywhere from 2 to 5 minutes for students to compose a sentence, depending on their level.

5. When everyone has finished a sentence, papers should be passed to the person on the right again, and Steps 3 and 4 should be repeated, but with a new vocabulary word.
6. Depending on the speed and skill of the students, you may want to have them write somewhere between 5 and 10 sentences.
7. When you come to the last sentence, be sure to tell the students it is the final one, so they can put some kind of conclusion on the story.
8. Collect all the papers and read out the stories one by one. (In a large class, you may wish to read just a few stories out loud and post the rest on the walls for a few days.) You and your students will be amazed at their humor and creativity. In addition, all the students get to hear a story about themselves.
9. After reading the stories, hand them back to the original writers.

Contributor

Kelly Fowler is Language Instructor at the Pan Intercultural Academy of Municipalities in Otsu City, Japan.

Retelling a Story From Different Perspectives

Levels
High intermediate +

Aims
Practice descriptive
writing and telling a
story

Class Time
40 minutes

Resources
Short newspaper
accounts of interesting
events, with enough
copies for each member
of the class

This activity helps develop students' creative writing about a real event. Students will describe the event from different points of view based on roles they choose. For example, if a news story is about a traffic accident, students will write about it from the point of view of the driver, a police officer, a pedestrian, and the passengers. If the story is about a burglary, the students will write from the viewpoint of the home owner, an eye witness and the detective. The students can develop or reconstruct the details as appropriate to their chosen roles. This serves as the starting point and may move on to the writing in different styles.

Procedure

1. Hand out a copy of a suitable newspaper story to each student. Ask them to read it silently. When appropriate, give the students the relevant background to the incident and explain vocabulary as necessary.
2. Explain the task to the students: They have to write an account of the story from the perspective of one of the persons involved. Different students in the class will choose different perspectives. Ask students to suggest who might be the writers of the different versions of the story. Put their suggestions on the board. Ask students to select one of the roles and begin to think of their own story version.
3. Brainstorm with the class on what the reactions might be of each of the people involved in the incident. Elicit as many ideas and suggestions as possible.
4. Now ask students to start writing about the event from the point of view of the role they have chosen, and to make rough notes on the type of information they will include in the story. Move around and give suggestions as needed.

5. Ask students to write the first draft of the story. Arrange the students into different groups according to the role they play. For example, all the drivers will form one group, all the police officers will form another group, and so on. (If the group is too big, form further subgroups). Within each group, exchange and compare the drafts in terms of the information included and the clarity of the event.
6. Have students individually revise their drafts. Give feedback when needed.
7. (optional) Invite some of the students to read their stories aloud.
8. Have students exchange papers with another group and read a story written by someone from a different perspective (e.g., a student taking the role of the driver in a traffic accident will read the story written by another student taking the role of the police officer).
9. Ask the students to compare the different stories written by a single group: how are they similar and different, what information is included in one but not the other, and whether this makes the story more effective. Pay special attention to the use of tense and connectives.

Contributor

Teresa Loh teaches in the Department of English of the City University of Hong Kong.

What Happens Next?

Levels
High intermediate +

Aims
Write a set of short
stories on a given theme
Focus on sentence-level
structure, vocabulary,
and editing

Class Time
1 hour

Resources
Lined paper and pens
List of vocabulary

Procedure

This example uses Christmas as a theme. It could just as easily be New Year's, Valentine's Day, spring, fairy tales, or some other theme.

1. (Done before the writing activity, even the day before.) The students read the poem *T'was the Night Before Christmas,* by Clement Moore, or some other seasonal poem or story. Then they discuss how they celebrate Christmas, or how they see others celebrate the holiday. Next they generate a list of words used in association with this topic. Words may include: *Santa, star, presents, tree, carol, snow, North Pole, and more.* Write this list on the board.

2. Ask students for examples of opening lines to a story with a Christmas (or winter) theme. Then ask them to write the opening line for such a story, using, if they chose, vocabulary from the list they generated previously. Circulate, helping and giving suggestions when asked.

3. Have students then pass the paper to their neighbor to the right (assuming they are sitting in a circle). The next student reads the opening and under it, writes the next line of the story. The students should be reminded to continue the story, watching for tenses, names, vocabulary used, and other details. They can also be encouraged to write longer sentences (both in content and complexity), and to be as wild and imaginative as possible.

4. When the second sentence is completed, the students fold back the first (opening) sentence so that only the second sentence can be read, and pass the story on to the right. Then the procedure is continued, with the students only able to read the line just above in the story, before writing the next line.

5. As you circulate, facilitate the writing. If there is a bottleneck (some-body being too creative), papers could be redistributed to those stu-

167

dents who already finished their turn. When 10 (or more) lines have been written, tell the students that the next line will be the conclusion and to finish up the story.

6. Have students unfold the stories and read them. Then, with a partner, they correct the stories (tense, agreement, prepositions and other things) in order to make the story flow smoothly. Favorite stories could then be read aloud, or rewritten and posted on the wall. They also make a good souvenir of the class because everyone contributed to the stories.

Caveats and Options

1. You should be quite active in facilitating the movement of papers and providing assistance, encouragement, and examples when needed.
2. This could be done with a grammar focus. For example, you could provide a conjunctive adverb (e.g., *therefore, nonetheless, however*) for the students to use correctly with each fold of the paper (extremely challenging).
3. This activity could be done without folding the paper over. However, one of the bonuses of this activity is that it is fast paced and interactive. It will slow down very quickly if students have to read all of what has been written before continuing the story.
4. If the class has more than 15 students, two groups may be preferable, and Steps 1 and 6 of the procedure could be done on different days.

Contributor

Cynthia Jones is with the Pacific Language Institute in Vancouver, British Columbia, Canada.

Write From the Start With Wordless Books

Levels
Beginning

Aims
Collectively write a
story based on the
pictures in a wordless
book

Class Time
45 minutes +

Resources
One different wordless
book for each group of
three students

With their limited vocabulary and command of the language, beginning students find it difficult to engage in writing that is meaningful and not formulaic. This activity gives each group of students the chance to pool their knowledge and write without being overly concerned with correctness. They are able to orally develop their story, write it, and finally, read it to another group.

Procedure

1. Divide the class into groups of three, either randomly or with a mix of ability level in each group. Give a different wordless book to each group.
2. Have the students in each group go through their book and begin talking to one another about what is happening in the story. At this point they are often producing one- or two-word phrases. They will ask you when they need a word to explain what is happening in the story.
3. When a group has finished their book, have them take out one piece of paper on which the group will collectively write their story. Each student should be encouraged to take a turn writing as the group works together to compose their story. They should be concentrating on conveying their meaning rather than worrying about mechanical correctness.
4. Once they have completed their story they should take turns reading the story to each other within their group. After each group has done this, students within each group should be assigned numbers from one to three. If the groups are arranged in a loosely circular fashion, the next step is easier. The students numbered 1 from each group will then take the group's story and the wordless book and go to the

169

neighboring group and read the story while the Number 2 students to whom they are reading try to follow the pictures in the book. Number 1 students read their stories to two or three groups and then the Number 2 students read to two or three groups starting in the circle of groups where student number 1 from their group left off. Finally, the Numbered 3 students from each group will pick up in the circle where student two from their group finished and read to the remaining groups.

Caveats and Options

This activity gives students the opportunity to speak, read, write, and listen in a cooperative, collaborative environment without feeling much anxiety. It also gives them an immediate audience of their peers for their writing. Collecting the stories afterwards will give you some ideas of strengths and weaknesses.

References and Further Reading

Smallwood, B. A. (1991). *The literature connection: A read-aloud guide for multicultural classrooms.* Reading, MA: Addison-Wesley.

Trelease, J. (1989). *The new read-aloud handbook.* New York: Penguin Books.

Contributor

Holbrook Mahn, currently enrolled in the TESOL doctoral program at the University of New Mexico, taught ESL at Belmont High School in Los Angeles for 3 years.

Prompted Write Around

Levels
Low intermediate +

Aims
Write at length without
being corrected

Class Time
20 minutes

Resources
Four sheets of lined
paper with one
sentence prompt

This task allows students to become so caught up in the activity that it becomes more like a game than a writing task. Students usually find it fun and tend to be very creative. This task could be used as a warm-up activity.

Procedure

1. Divide the students into groups of four.
2. Give each student in the group a piece of paper with a different prompt written at the top. There should be one prompt for each student in the group. Four possible prompts that could be used are:

- There are many good jobs in my home country.
- I hope to get a good job someday.
- I like being in America.
- America is a very strange place.

Give the students plenty of room to write and to be creative. It is important to remember that the prompts could be any type of sentence and could focus on any particular point. For example, if the past tense is being taught, the prompt could be in the past tense.

3. Instruct the students to write sentences based on the previous sentences.
4. Give the students 5–7 minutes to write and then instruct them to switch. If the student is in the middle of a sentence, they should stop at that point. Each paper is then rotated to the right, where the student must then read what has been written thus far, and continue writing the essay from where the last student stopped writing.
5. Give each student the opportunity to write about each of the four prompts at least once.

Contributor

Thomas Nixon teaches in the American English Institute at California State University, Fresno, in the United States.

A Typical Day, Revisited

Levels
Beginning–intermediate

Aims
Describe daily routines

Class Time
10–15 minutes

Resources
Picture of a person, especially one involved in an occupation
Chalkboard or overhead projector (OHP)

Descriptions of daily routine are standard fare in low-level classes. They are especially helpful in giving natural opportunities to practice habitual verbs. However, once the students have described the daily routine of, typically, John the salesman or Mary the student and their own daily routine, they still need further practice with this discourse function and its associated grammar. This technique allows more scope for the students' imagination, and encourages students to use their culturally specific knowledge and wider vocabulary. Thus, the exercise can be repeated many times without becoming boring.

Procedure

1. Do usual assignments, for example, John's Daily Activities or My Day. Point out grammatical features of subject-verb agreement, and present/ past habitual verbs.
2. Find an intriguing picture, especially showing someone involved in an occupational or culturally specific task. You can also use a Godzilla toy or other imaginary creature. The use of different pictures elicits different gender and number. (For example, the addition of two baby Godzillas to the adult one often results in a gender shift of Godzilla from male to female.)

3. Using one picture or model as an example, with the whole class, orally elicit the beginning of the daily activities, for example, *"Every day—When does Godzilla get up?... First light? Dawn, yes, ok, and what does he eat for breakfast?..."* You can also do this on the board or OHP as a group writing.
4. You can ask students to finish this one individually in class, or at home. Or, you can ask students to choose their own picture and write several paragraphs on that person or animal's daily activities.
5. You or the writers can read aloud several of the resulting compositions, after revision and correction.

Caveats and Options

Ask students to bring a picture of someone from the students' cultural background; or a picture or model of an animal that students have background knowledge.

Appendix: Two Sample Texts

Tang Li Chuen is a star in the Chinese Opera. Every day, she gets up at 2 p.m. She eats a big breakfast of noodles with steamed pork and spinach, and then goes to the theater. She practices with the other actors. Then she gets into her beautiful, colorful costume. Then she puts on her makeup. This takes three hours. The show starts at 8 p.m. She is nervous but she goes on stage . . . .

Godzilla lives in a nice comfortable cave near the ocean. He gets up every day at dawn, and goes to the beach to swim and catch fish. He eats about 200 pounds of fish for breakfast. Every other day he also eats some electricity from the high-power lines. On weekdays he goes to the movie studio to work on his new movie. He rehearses very hard all morning. He usually eats lunch with Mothra, Gamera and the Peanuts. Even though in the movies they are all enemies, they are really good friends . . . .

Acknowledgment

Takae Tsujioka drew the illustration of Godzilla.

Contributor

Lise Winer teaches at the Department of Linguistics, Southern Illinois University, Carbondale, in the United States.

◆ Fables and Proverbs
Fables

Levels
Intermediate +

Aims
Describe actions
Instruct others

Class Time
1 hour

Resources
Copies of a collection of
fables (see References
and Further Reading)

This activity encourages students to use their familiarity with their culture's fables to create one of their own. The structure of a fable provides a framework for composition but still gives the author almost complete freedom in the creation of a message and the characters and circumstances that will convey the message. You may wish to direct that creativity by requiring that certain structures be included in the text. The results of this activity can be used later as reading texts or topics of discussion.

Procedure

1. Have students read three or four selected fables.
2. As a class, determine the characteristics of a fable:
   - It conveys a principle of behavior through an analogy of fictitious but plausible actions.
   - The main characters are animals, inanimate objects, gods, or men and women.
   - It is brief.
   - There is a moral that may or may not be stated.

3. Ask students to create an original fable. They will have to decide what the moral of their fable will be, what characters would be appropriate to convey that idea, how the story will develop to illustrate the moral and what sort of language will be used. This may be done as either an in-class or out-of-class activity.
4. If desired, students working in pairs can suggest improvements or corrections of the rough drafts.
5. For a subsequent session, make copies of each fable. The students can either simply enjoy reading their classmates' creations or as a

References and Further Reading

Appendix: Sample Fables Written by Students

continuation, students can publish a classroom collection of fables, complete with illustrations.

1. There are many fables to choose from. Some possibilities include Aesop's "The Tortoise and the Hare," "The Lion and the Mouse," "The Goose and the Golden Eggs," "The Town Mouse and the Country Mouse;" and Jean de la Fontaine's "The Crow and the Fox" and "The Cobbler and the Banker."
2. Other known fablists include: John Gay, Gotthold Lessing, Ivan Kriloff, Hitopadesa and Jean Pierre de Florian.

How the Rhinoceros Lost His Color

Once upon a time there was a rhinoceros of many colors. His head was red, his legs were yellow and his feet were purple. This rhinoceros liked to look at the flower design on his bedspread. He loved this design very much and after a time he stayed in bed all day long and looked at the pretty flowers in rows straight and neat.

One day his neighbor paid him a visit. The neighbor invited the rhinoceros to take a walk in the woods. The rhinoceros accompanied him. Hid didn't like the disorder of the woods, he ardently wanted his neat, orderly bedspread. When he returned to his house he jumped right in his bed and he never got out. It took all his colors and he became forever gray and fat.

The moral is: One can have too much order. (Alison Hart)

The Octopus and the Angelfish

The octopus prefers to stay at the bottom of the ocean. She hides in the crevices of the rocks. She squirts black ink at her enemies. She seems disagreeable and contemptible.

The Angelfish is very exuberant. He is very colorful, but he is also pretentious. One day, the angelfish traveled to the bottom of the ocean. There, he saw the octopus who was hiding in a cranny in the rock. The angelfish presumed that the octopus was dangerous, so the angelfish left the bottom of the ocean. The octopus was very sad. He thought that the angelfish was very beautiful. Because the angelfish was curious, he traveled to the bottom of the ocean again. This time the octopus wasn't in a crevice of a rock. She was walking on the ocean floor. She was crying.

"Why are you crying?" asked the angelfish, curiously.

"Because I don't have any friends. Everyone thinks that I am dangerous," the octopus said.

"You hide in the crevices of rocks all the time," the angelfish responded.

"I'm not hiding. I'm just shy."

"I'm sorry," the angelfish said, "Next time, I'm not going to assume the worst. Anyway, will you be my friend?"

"Of course, I thought you would never ask." (Cathy Fisher)

The Weeping Willow

Why, weeping willow
Are you crying?
What has happened?
Are you sad?
What are you doing
With your life?
I am the weeping willow
I cry because
It is my penance.
But, why this penance
Have you a sin
With God?
Yes, I have sinned
But I was not
Always a tree.
I was a man
Who was a sinner

This is my penance.
God said "No!"
But I disobeyed
Now, I have all the pain
I must forever weep. (Kandice Griffey)

Contributor

Clarine Beatty is currently pursuing an MA in French at Pennsylvania State University, in the United States.

What's the Real Story?

Levels
Any

Aims
Differentiate the stated
facts from the implied
meaning
Understand
chronological order as
used in narration
Realize that all cultures
try to teach values
through writing

Class Time
40 minutes +

Resources
Copy of a fairy tale at
the appropriate skill
level

Student writers need to learn that good writing effectively conveys the writer's ideas, and that the writing is more effective if it is packaged well.

Procedure

1. Read aloud a classic fairy tale such as *Little Red Riding Hood*.
2. After you have finished reading the fairy tale, have the students list in chronological order the events that took place. Encourage them to give as many details as they can.
3. As a class go over the details that they have listed. Have the students write the details on the board. Encourage students to add facts they think belong any place on the list.
4. Discuss whether they think that the chronological order of events is really the most important idea of the story. (In other words, do they think that the author wrote the story to convey the details that they have listed chronologically?)
5. Discuss what they think the main idea of the story really is. Talk about the idea of a moral. Ask what they think the fairy tale teaches us. (For example, *Little Red Riding Hood* teaches children the importance of listening to their mothers.)
6. Go back over the fairy tale and have the students point out each place where they think there was an implied message to the listener to behave in a certain way. (For example, Mother said, "Go directly to your grandmother's house.")

Caveats and Options

1. Have the students pick a fairy tale that is popular in their culture. Ask them to do the following:

- Relate the story in detailed chronological order making sure to use appropriate transitions and details.
- Write a paragraph that explains what the fairy tale is supposed to teach children.

2. During the next class, discuss fairy tales that the students have written. Have students try to guess what they think the moral is before the student reads his paragraph explaining what the moral is.
3. Options for intermediate to advanced students:

- Discuss the concept of satire. Perhaps use Swift's "A Modest Proposal."
- Discuss as a group problems that the students see in the world. Have each student isolate one problem that he would like to see changed. Ask the students to try to write a fairly simple children's story where they never state the moral but know that the readers will infer it.

Contributor

Arlene Bublick teaches ESL in the intensive and part-time programs at William Rainey Harper College, Palatine, Illinois, in the United States.

The Proverb

Levels
Advanced; adult
education

Aims
Narrate a story

Class Time
1 1/2 hours

Resources
Handout with proverbs
(see Appendix)

Students are able to relate to proverbs that express the same ideas in their own language and then transfer this knowledge into an essay.

Procedure

1. Read each proverb in a large-group setting, and explain proverbs that students do not understand.
2. Discuss whether the students' languages contain proverbs that express the same ideas as those listed.
3. After completing the list, discuss which proverbs are similar or opposite in meaning and which are the students' favorite proverbs in their language.
4. Ask students to volunteer a time when they experienced a particular proverb.
5. Have students draft an essay on the experiences, incorporating the proverb.

Acknowledgments

Rima Katz is the source of the proverb list in the Appendix.

References and Further Reading

The concise Oxford dictionary of proverbs. (1982). Oxford: Oxford University Press.

Appendix: Sample Proverbs

Does your language contain proverbs that express the same ideas as those below? Here are some common American proverbs:

1. People in glass houses shouldn't throw stones.
2. The other man's grass is always greener.
3. Let sleeping dogs lie.
4. A barking dog seldom bites.
5. Two heads are better than one.
6. All that glitters is not gold.
7. Many hands make light work.
8. You can't judge a book by its cover.
9. Beauty is only skin deep.
10. A bird in the hand is worth two in the bush.
11. Silence is golden.
12. All work and no play make Jack a dull boy.
13. Early to bed and early to rise make a man healthy, wealthy, and wise.
14. The early bird catches the worm.
15. Better late than never.

Which proverbs are similar in meaning?
Which proverbs seem to have opposite meanings?
Do you have any favorite proverbs in your native language?

Contributor

Constance Colon-Jones teaches in the Speech Communications Department at Pennsylvania State University, in the United States.

Teaching Writing Through Fables and Proverbs

Levels
Intermediate

Aims
Illustrate a point
Identify main ideas
Assess suitability of
supporting details

Class Time
Two 1-hour sessions

Resources
Proverbs written on
strips of paper, then cut
in half
Peer review sheet (see
Appendix)

In this activity students get practice in working with the notions of main idea and supporting details. In addition, they can experiment creatively with ways to illustrate a point. The drafting, feedback, revision, and rewriting stages help students to build their writing strategies and view writing as a manageable process. All the while, the students are working collaboratively and practicing listening, speaking, reading and writing language skills.

Procedure

Lesson 1

1. Preteach the past tense.
2. Write out proverbs on slips of paper and cut in the middle.
3. Write a proverb on the board (e.g., Slow but steady wins the race) and tell students a fable such as "The Tortoise and the Hare." Ask them what is meant by the proverb.
4. Tell students that we use many proverbs which are often found in informal speech and, with some variations, newspaper headlines. Give one more example and ask them to tell you what it means.
5. Brainstorm proverbs that they know from their countries and list them on the board (e.g., From China: "Marriages are made in Hell.")
6. Give one half of each proverb to each student. Tell students to circulate, look for their matching half and then sit down.
7. Have pairs report their proverb to the group and try to explain what it means.
8. Tell pairs to write a short fable (one page long) to illustrate the meaning of the proverb. Students must not mention the proverb in their fable. Give the students the options to use a proverb from their own countries or to work individually.

Lesson 2

1. Have students list their proverbs on the board.
2. Have students attach peer feedback sheet (see Appendix) to fables and pass to teacher. Redistribute stories to individuals or pairs for reading and responding.
3. After three people or pairs have responded, give papers back to students. Have students revise and rewrite their fables, based on the feedback received.
4. Follow up these lessons with more work on main idea and supporting details.

Caveats and Options

1. Teachers should allow for individual learning style differences and permit students to work alone if they wish. Students should also be allowed to work with proverbs from their own countries instead of those offered by the teacher. This flexibility validates our students' cultural backgrounds and personal experiences.
2. Give the students the options

   - to use a proverb from their own countries and
   - to work individually.

Appendix: Peer Response Handout

1. What did you like most about this story? Why?
2. What did you like least about this story? Why?
3. What proverb does this story illustrate? Was it easy or difficult to guess? Why?
4. What part of the fable gave you the best clue to the proverb?
5. Were there any parts of the story that seemed unnecessary? If so, underline them for the author(s).
6. Look for all past tense verbs. Are they used correctly? If not, circle them.

Contributor

Helen Raptis is an instructor at Camosun College, Victoria, Canada.

◆ Biography
Paired Biography

Levels
Intermediate +

Aims
Write a short biography
that accurately
introduces one other
member of the class

Class Time
40–50 minutes

Resources
Collection of interview
questions generated by
the students
Chalkboard

The idea here is to practice the use of the past, present perfect, and progressive in the context of an activity that involves the exchange of personally relevant information and will contribute to a sense of community in the class. It could begin a series of lessons in which students use the biographies as the basis of editing exercises.

Procedure

1. Tell the students they will be interviewing each other with the purpose of writing a short biographical essay about their partner. Invite students to suggest questions they would ask someone whom they wanted to get to know.
2. Write suggested questions on the board.
3. After all the questions have been generated, identify any grammar mistakes they contain. Then work with the students to explain what is incorrect and repair the mistakes.
4. Pair each student with a partner and ask them to interview each other, using the questions on the board. Advanced students may include additional questions they think of during the interview process.
5. As soon as students have the information, discuss the best order in which to present it.
6. In a subsequent session, or at home, have students write up the information about their partner in the form of a short biography.
7. Conclude the activity by having each student read the biography to a small group or the class, depending on class size.
8. (Optional) Have students edit their essays for grammatical errors (e.g., subject-verb agreement).

Contributor

Terri Cononelos is a doctoral student in the Second Language Acquisition and Teaching Program at the University of Arizona, in the United States.

Creative Book Reports

Levels
Intermediate +

Aims
Entertain imaginatively

Class Time
Several hours

Resources
Wide assortment of book covers (fiction only)

Quite often, both teachers and texts are guilty of highly repetitive activity types. This activity adds some variety to the assignments of the week. What better way to realize "writing as a thinking process" than to ask students to write a book report for a book which they have not yet read.

Procedure

1. Contact the staff of a local library to obtain some of the book jackets (normally thrown away when libraries catalogue and shelve new acquisitions). Collect a variety of fiction covers (about twice as many as there are students in your class. (Laminating them is an optional step.)
2. Bring your collection of covers to class and spread them all out on a desk.
3. Invite students to come forward (row by row if necessary) and browse through the covers. Ask them to pick one that seems interesting to them. When they have returned to their seats, you can introduce and explain the popular saying, "Don't judge a book by its cover." Then tell them that although you may not judge, you can certainly write a report. Now that you have their interest, tell them that this is an exercise in creative writing. They are to pretend they have read the book and are being assigned to write a book report just like those on the board.
4. Students may use the remainder of the class period to brainstorm, or you may assign this first prewriting stage for homework. Follow-up stages may differ depending on your personal model of the writing process and whether your students enjoy peer review procedures
5. Set a due date at which time students bring their book cover and report. Each student mounts the two on poster board and displays it

in the classroom. Students may roam around the room reading a couple of their fellow students' creative work.

6. At some future point you may evaluate them. You might also involve the class in this procedure, awarding prizes to the few who received the most votes.

7. The first time around results in many colorless, bland reports. Quite often students are not used to creative writing, even in their own language. There will be a few examples, however, that will open their eyes to the possibilities, and future attempts to use this procedure will result in more creative work.

Contributor

Mark James teaches at Brigham Young University, Hawaii, in the United States.

Evaluative Writing Through Film Reviews

Levels
Advanced

Aims
Develop critical writing,
analysis, and evaluation
skills

Class Time
Several lessons

Resources
Film of significant
social/cultural impact
(e.g., *Malcolm X* or
Stand and Deliver)
Favorable and
unfavorable reviews of
the film
Viewing equipment

This activity helps students develop a critical eye and learn the basic concepts that underlie evaluative writing that is authoritative, persuasive, organized, well reasoned. The activity is good preparation for preacademic students who may be asked to do similar assignments in their college courses.

Procedure

1. Students read and discuss a favorable and unfavorable review of the selected film as supplied from the print media. The teacher pays special attention to the main points made in each review, its reasoning, organization, and vocabulary of critical writing. This helps to spark interest in the film among the students.
2. Students then view the film as a group.
3. Afterwards, divide students into five groups and discuss for 10–15 minutes one of several basic categories used to evaluate the film. These include:

   - Characters: What made them believable, unbelievable?
   - Music: How did it establish or support the film's message, style, mood?
   - Message: What did you learn from watching this film?
   - Style: Was the film humorous, sad, witty, confusing?
   - Form: Was the film visually picturesque, strange, gritty, urban, dark?

4. Give group secretaries a sheet with one of these five elements written on top. Their task is to record the comments (including conflicting ones) of group members during the discussion.
5. The group then exchanges its sheet with another group who has yet to see this category. After each exchange, groups discuss and record

their comments on the sheet below the comments of the previous group(s). The exchange continues until all five groups have seen each category sheet.

6. Collect and copy all five sheets for the entire class.

7. Using these student-generated comments, ask everyone to write a film review. The format below is one example that has the essential elements of a good film review.

- Write a short introduction to the film including a brief summary.
- Analyze the film in terms of each element but use details (dialogue, story occurrences). from the film to support your opinion.
- Consider any opposing arguments to your conclusions and refute them.
- Give your own recommendations.

8. After students write their own film reviews, copy the best ones for the benefit of the entire class. You may also discuss the good and bad points (e.g., flaws in logic, effective argumentative style) for some of these reviews.

Contributor

Phil Plourde has an MA in Linguistics from Ohio University and is an ESL instructor at the Center for English as a Second Language, Southern Illinois University, Carbondale, Illinois.

Art Field Trip

Levels
Beginning +

Aims
Describe different kinds
of art works in terms of
form, line color, texture,
composition and media
Express the reasons for
liking particular pieces
of art

Class Time
Two 50-minute sessions
and 15 minutes for
vocabulary preview

Resources
Community or
university art exhibit to
serve as the focus of the
field trip
Note-taking guide (see
Appendix)

This exercise exposes students to the artistic expression of the host culture as well as to the vocabulary with which to describe scenes, situations, and objects found in the art work. The students give reasons for their choices of three of the pieces of their essay beyond simply liking them.

Procedure

Day 1

1. Give students the note-taking guide handout on the day before the field trip. Go over some of the terms, illustrating them when possible. (Some terms, such as those for different media, will not be clear until examples are viewed on the field trip.) Students must bring this handout on the field trip.
2. Tell the students that they will be writing an essay about the three pieces of art in the exhibit that they like best. (This is a good time to review the form of the essay: introduction, thesis statement, topic sentences, support, conclusion).

Day 2

1. Guide students throughout the art exhibit. Describe different kinds of art, taking care to draw the students' attention to a wide variety of media and style. (If you preview the exhibit, you will be able to avoid pieces that deal with subjects that might prove sensitive for some students.) Encourage students to ask questions, speculate about the artists' intentions, and manipulate the descriptive language. Draw attention to the name of the artist and the title of the work so that students can refer to the piece correctly in their writing.

2. After about 30 minutes, the students should be allowed to reexamine the pieces on their own in order to choose the three they like best for their essays.

Day 3

1. Using their note-taking guides, the students write a composition describing the three pieces of art that they like best. Their concluding paragraph should tell which piece was their favorite and why.

Appendix: Note-Taking Guide for Art Field Trip

Instructions: Choose three works of art to write about.

1.

   Artist
   Title
   Date
   Media

2.
3.

Take notes on each piece as the tour guide describes them. You can indicate the words that apply to each piece by placing 1, 2 or 3 next to the words used to describe each one in the list below.

Two Dimensional	Three Dimensional	General
oil painting	sculpture	figure
water color	totem	form
oil crayon	vessel	shape
ink	ceramic	circular
woodcut	glaze	oval
graphite	texture	round
etching	rough	square
lithograph	smooth	rectangular
mixed media	patterned	triangular
landscape	metal	curved
portrait	steel	realistic
still life	brass	abstract
line	copper	symmetrical
thick	aluminum	asymmetrical
hand-made paper	welded	picture plane
fibers	forged	movement

Contributor

Beverly Walker-Watkins is Instructor of English and Fine Art in the Department of Humanities, Allegany Community College, Maryland, in the United States.

♦ Poetry and Verse
Painting With Words

Levels
Beginning +

Aims
Describe chosen images
Rearrange lexical items

Class Time
60–90 minutes

Resources
Short poem with a high
content of collocation
Collection of visuals
relating to the poem
(e.g., seed catalogue,
set of perfume
advertisements, scissors,
glue, paper, biodata
relating to the poem)

The idea is to encourage students to experiment with a text type they are unfamiliar with, regard as intrinsically difficult, or may have reservations about. The visual prompts help to free the students from their own imagery. In the second stage, the visuals serve as a stimulus for a word search. This is particularly effective with younger adults who have difficulty convincing themselves that they can say what they really want to in English. This activity provides a way for the students to gain confidence in ownership of the language.

Procedure

1. Invite students to think of an everyday activity that they enjoy, then to daydream a little to make it even more enjoyable. Remind them that everybody fantasies very easily. Then hand them a poem rich in high frequency nouns.
2. Focusing on the noun content of the poem, present the students with a range of visuals from which they may select the pictures they think most closely represent the nouns in the poem. They are then free to cut up the poem into suitable phrases or lines and mount the appropriate visual onto one section of the folded paper.
3. Each student now has a colorful text and visuals collage to which they are free to add further visuals that they have noticed while selecting those in Step 2.
4. Make yourself available, together with other students, to act as a resource for the words needed to describe the second set of visuals. These are assembled on the remaining half of the miniposters in a similar pattern to that of the original poem. Some students will follow this closely and others will be more willing to make departures.

5. Direct the students' attention to the writer of the original poem and ask who the poet is now. Most students will be surprised that the text they have generated is indeed a poem.

6. Following the original poet's biodata, encourage students to write biodata for each other. Display the posters as appropriate for the institution.

Appendix: Sample Poem

On the back of *Cosmopolitan*

A girl kissed lips of stone
To advertise a perfume. Fear
Of living life alone

Had driven her to it
And her safety was the thing
That made a dull cold statue
More attractive than a king.

Contributors

Liz Clarkson and Sean Power work at the Bell Education Trust in Geneva, Switzerland.

Beginnings to Poetry Writing

Levels
Any

Aims
Explore and build images from own writing

Class Time
10 minutes/poem

Resources
2–3 minutes of evocative instrumental music
One piece of paper for each student with one *wh*-question word on it

For many learners, creative writing exercises, especially those using poetry, can be disappointing when they read their results. This activity guarantees success because each person is responsible for only one line, and the final poem is a group effort. Also because poetry can be freer than prose, this one line can easily be a sentence fragment.

Procedure

1. Divide students into small groups. Each student gets one question card with one wh-question on it. For lower level classes use only *who, what, where,* and *when* because they are easier to answer than *how* and *why*. Higher level students in a group could get two question cards.

2. Explain to students that they are to write the answer to the question word on their card as it applies to the piece of music they are listening to. Emphasize that you only want only short sentences or fragments for answers. (For example, the student with the question *Where* is encouraged to think of answers to questions like *Where is this music playing?* Answers could range from *a winter morning in Paris, in my canoe under the stars,* to *this is a country for old people.*)

3. Dim the lights and play the piece several times. Students write their answers and the group organizes all the slips into a poem (or short story if they wrote a lot). Display each group's results and let everyone walk around the room reading while listening to the music again. At this time the audience could also make suggestions for titles.

Appendix: Student Examples

The following are examples from two groups in classes of differing ability. Both are based on the same piece of music of Peruvian music.

No Title

Every holiday time
In my small village
Under the tallest tree in the village
The women are dancing

Happiness

In a small Indian village
The little girl, living in a small village at the foot of the mountain, puts on a colorful cloth
Everybody makes a big circle and dances cheerfully
When a big battle is over

Contributor

Van Le is Language Instructor at the Japan Intercultural Academy of Municipalities, Otsu-shi, Japan.

Musical Stream of Consciousness

Levels
Intermediate +

Aims
Write expressively

Class Time
40 minutes

Resources
Folk music

This activity makes students aware of their ability to write expressively by producing short prose poems.

Procedure

1. Tell students that they are going to hear a short piece of music. Tell them that you want them to relax and allow their minds to conjure up images and associations suggested by the music they are going to hear.
2. Tell the students to rest their heads on their arms and close their eyes.
3. Play an extract of some evocative music (no singing), for example, some melancholy Irish folk music.
4. When you have faded out the music, ask the students to write down words and phrases that conjure up the feeling they had when they were listening to the music. Emphasize that you do not want them to write connected sentences, only random words and phrases.
5. When they have done this, put students into threes and ask them to share what they have written down.
6. Then ask the students in their groups of three to select and combine their words and phrases, expanding or changing them if they want to. Their task is to produce a three-line prose poem. Monitor their work at this point, making suggestions and encouraging students to make unusual collocations and sentence combinations.
7. When all groups have finished, organize a choral reading of all the poems, one group of three reading their "poem" followed by another group of three and so on. Turn off the lights or draw the blinds to create additional atmosphere.
8. Collect all the poems and arrange them as verses of a longer class poem. This class poem can be photocopied and distributed next lesson so that the each member of the class has ownership of a class created poem.

**Appendix:
Sample Class
Poem**

Through A Tunnel of Dead Leaves

Solemn is the place,
Fear is in my heart,
Who will be my lamppost in the dark?

I wonder round this holy place,
Searching for something.
A chalice, a chalice?

I do not know.
I wonder round this Holy Place,
Searching, searching.

Death drifts towards me,
I feel helpless, hopeless, lonely.
Where can my soul hide?
Mysterious, endless dreams,
Spirits and angels pray over me,
I pray back with my eyes

But fox fairies bite holes in my dreams,
And fear wages its vendetta,
I don not want to die.
Through a tunnel of leaves
To a dimension of distant hope
I stumble.

The leaves are waving their hands,
The wind is whispering,
Praising the power of hope.
The distant voices of the dead call to me,
Their voices echo in this cold church.
Will the colours in my mind all be lost?

by BA TESL Students of the City University of Hong Kong

Contributor

Dino Mahoney is a Lecturer in the English Department of the City University of Hong Kong where he teaches on BA and MA TESL programs. He has also taught in London and Athens and was Director of Studies at the British Council in Dubai and Hong Kong.

Words Words Words Worth

Levels
Intermediate +

Aims
Use language creatively
through guided writing

Class Time
2 hours +

Resources
None

This activity was originally intended for and used in a poetry class for nonnative first-year English Literature-major students. Yet it can be adopted for language classes. Writing their own poems in various forms improves students' writing style and enhances their ability to use vocabulary creatively.

Procedure

1. Ask students to select a theme (e.g., love, hatred, war, peace, life, death) and have them write down as many words related to this theme as possible.
2. Ask students to write a poem of five lines, using words from their list. Have a few students read their poems aloud.
3. Briefly explain what rhyme means and ask students to try and make the lines in their five line poem rhyme with each other in any form they like (e.g., aabbccd, abcbd.) They may change the vocabulary, but should try to stick to the original list as much as possible. Have a few students read their poems aloud.
4. Explain what alliteration means and ask students to write an alliterative poem of five lines on the same theme. Again, they should try to keep to the original list as much as possible. Have a few students read their poems aloud.
5. Explain what a pattern poem is and ask students to write a pattern poem of five lines on the same theme, in any shape they like. They should keep as many of the words in the original list as possible. Have a few students read their poems aloud.
6. Have students read the poems in groups and let them choose the best one(s) in each group.

Caveats and Options

Repeat this procedure to include use of figurative language (e.g., metaphors, similes)

Contributor

Wisam Mansour, previously Assistant Professor of English Literature at Eastern Mediterranean University in Cyprus, works for the Ministry of Education in Jordan.

◆ Journals
Informal Diary Writing

Levels
Any

Aims
Develop fluency,
confidence and pleasure
in informal writing

Class Time
5 minutes +

Resources
Blank exercise book

Informal written English is more difficult to develop and practice than spoken informal English. Responsive diary writing provides an interface for the teacher and student to communicate regardless of language level.

Procedure

1. Introduce the idea of responsive diary writing by inviting the students to comment or expand their own opinions on a topic in the news or on a personal interest or concern.
2. Collect the diaries weekly, rotating whose you collect each time (a few for you to read each night/day). Read them and write your own responses in each individual diary. Questions posed afford further responses and engender a dialogue.
3. If the activity is sustained over a period of weeks, significant improvement in grammar and style are likely to be apparent.

Contributor

Norma Green is Senior Tutor and English for Academic Purposes Coordinator in the English Language Unit, at the University of Aberystwyth, Wales, in the United Kingdom.

◆ Descriptive Writing
Desert Island

Levels
Low intermediate

Aims
Describe route

Class Time
20–30 minutes

Resources
Handout with sample
passage (see Appendix)

The students have to describe a route for their partner. The activity includes an oral whole-class episode, followed by a writing exercise that has a controlled part and a free part.

Procedure

1. Ask the class to describe what they might find on a desert island and build up an island on the chalkboard.
2. Pair off students. Give each partner one half of the handout (see Appendix).
3. Each partner should describe where they have been by filling in the missing conjunctions. They then say where they are going, in their own words.
4. When they have finished, have them separate the note and their map and give the note to their partner.
5. Each partner then has to fill in their partner's route on their own map. They then check if the result is right.
6. Take in the notes to look at them.

Appendix: Sample Passage Handout

Fill in the blanks in the passage and then say where you are going:

Dear Friends,

Glad you are safe. We swam to the reef in the east _____ to the beach. _____ we climbed the mountain, _____ did not see anyone. _____ we came down here to the palm trees.

Now we are going _____

_____

_____

_____

_____

_____ .

Marking: 1st paragraph = 3
            2nd paragraph = 7

Fill in the blanks in the passage and then say where you are going:

Dear Classmates,

Welcome to the island! We reached the reef in the north _____
swam to the cliff. _____ we climbed the cliffs _____
crossed the hills. We went up the mountain, _____ didn't see
anyone. _____ we came down to the bay.

We are going

_____

_____

Marking: 1st paragraph = 3
            2nd paragraph = 7

Contributor

Anthony Bruton teaches in the Faculty of Philology, University of Seville, Spain.

A Guide to Your New Hometown

Levels
Low intermediate +

Aims
Inform fellow students
of entertainment and
leisure opportunities
around their new
hometown

Class Time
90 minutes

Resources
A model entry for the
Guide to Sydney (see
Appendix A)
Formatted handout for
students to complete
(see Appendix B)
Overhead transparency
of the formatted
handout
List of possible places to
visit collected on the
board

This activity was devised in response to several students' complaints that they didn't know any places in Sydney, Australia, where they could spend their free time. I was aware that they all had knowledge of some places that they would be able to share. These students were preparing to study in a variety of fields. The activity gave them the chance to write an informative text on a general topic rather than in their specialist areas. Later, we published a booklet and gave a copy to each student. After reading this booklet, another class compiled their own to distribute to our class.

Procedure

1. Show your model entry for *A Guidebook to Sydney* (see Appendix A). Read through each section of the entry discussing the kind of information presented. Also discuss the use of the simple present tense for description, imperative for instructions, and *can* and *could* for possible activities and things that you could take.
2. Invite the students to offer suggestions for other places to visit around Sydney (or your city) on the weekend. Write all of the suggestions on the board.
3. At this point, you may wish to jointly construct another entry with the class. Choose a well-known place, elicit the necessary information for each section of the entry from the class, and write it on a transparency.
4. Ask students to nominate which place they would like to write about. Students interested in writing about the same place can work in pairs if they wish.
5. Distribute the form listing the required sections (see Appendix B) for each entry. Using the form makes the entries uniform, a usual characteristic of this kind of information text.

6. Have students draft their entries.
7. Have students discuss their entries with a peer and make revisions if necessary.
8. Have students discuss their entries with you and revise if necessary.
9. Collate and reproduce all of the entries to make a booklet.

Appendix A: Model Entry for *A Guide to Sydney*

Place: Shelley Beach

Description: Shelley Beach is a small, beautiful beach approximately 20 minutes walk from Manly. It is protected, offering safe swimming for all the family.

Suburb: Manly

The best time to go there: Go on the weekend if you want to be with the crowds of "beautiful people," topless sunbathers, etc. Go during the week for a quieter time

How you can get there: Catch the Manly ferry or Jetcat from Circular Quay. The trip takes approximately 20–25 minutes. Shelley Beach is about a 20 minute walk from Manly Wharf.

What you can do there: You can go swimming, snorkeling and scuba diving. You can also go surfing at nearby Fairy Bower. You can do anything you normally do at the beach. Two restaurants are open for lunch and dinner. They're not cheap. You can also buy ice creams and drinks from nearby shops.

What to take: Take your swimming costume, towel and factor 15+ sun screen. There is not a lot of protection from the sun so wear a hat. You could take a picnic if you plan to make a day of it or get some take-away in Manly.

Costs: Free

Contributed by: Tony

Appendix B: A Guide to Leisure in

Place

Description

Suburb

Best time to get there

What you can do there

Costs

Contributor

Anthony Butterworth teaches for the Adult Migrant English Service, New South Wales, Australia.

Who Are They?

Levels
Beginning +

Aims
Describe an individual

Class Time
Two 50-minute sessions

Resources
Colored magazine
pictures of people
Handout, notes, or
pictures in their book of
vocabulary for body
parts and items of
clothing
Piece of paper and
writing implement

In this activity, learners use language that they have previously studied in class. They see the importance of accuracy and detail in their descriptions and must use listening, speaking, and social skills.

Procedure

1. Have learners form groups of whatever size is most convenient for your class; three learners to a group works well. Give each group a number.
2. Ask each group to send one member up to the front of the class to choose a picture from those spread on the table. Tell the class that the pictures are secret and should only be shown to group members.
3. Ask the groups to write a description of the person in their picture; note that you will collect one text for the whole group. Learners should invent a name for the person and include it in their texts. They should only describe the clothing and important physical characteristics of the person; they should not explain what the person is doing or where the person is. As they write, rotate throughout the groups noting problems with the texts and discussing these with group members.
4. Learners should write their group number on the picture and the text; you should then collect them.
5. Read the texts aloud, writing the names that the learners have chosen on the board. While the text is being read, each learner should take notes. They should not write everything (the first text could be used as an example for a brief discussion of note-taking). For beginners, read each text two or three times.
6. Give learners some time to compare notes with their group. During this time, set the pictures up in the front of the room. If it is a very

large class, the pictures may be circulated with a time limit or posted on the walls about the classroom.

7. Ask learners to write the numbers 1–10 on their papers. Explain that they must use their notes to assign the proper name to each of the individuals in the pictures. Learners should write the name of the individual after the number on their paper which corresponds to the one on the picture. This part of the activity could be arranged as a competition, but learners are usually sufficiently motivated to solve the puzzle that it need not be.

8. Ask groups to explain their answers to the class, using examples from their notes to discuss which clues were important in attaching the name to the individual.

9. This activity could conclude by your asking groups to say how many names they attached correctly and assigning a winner. It could also be extended by discussing the importance to writing of clarity and the careful choice of details, and asking groups to revise or improve their texts. As a follow-up, learners could be asked to apply the knowledge gained through this activity by describing themselves, someone they know, or someone famous. These texts could be hung on the wall for learners to guess the name of the individual being described.

Caveats and Options

For more advanced classes, pictures that include only one gender make this exercise more difficult.

Contributor

Joy Egbert teaches in northern Idaho and Washington state.

Recipe Writing

Levels
Beginning +

Aims
Practice taking notes
Practice a different form
of writing
Promote cultural
integration and
understanding

Class Time
30 minutes/recipe/
group

Resources
Ingredients and utensils
for recipe

This activity gets students interacting and writing while they exchange cultural information.

Procedure

1. Divide the students into national or ethnic groups a couple of days before the activity is to be done.
2. Ask them to make a dish representative of their culture.
3. Then with utensils handy (e.g., knives, bowls), each group explains how to make their dish. The classmates are to write down the recipe as they hear the instructions. They can also participate in the preparation of it.
4. Ask the students to hand their notes in to the group explaining the recipe. The group must then correct the recipes both grammatically and stylistically and return them to the students the following day.
5. When all groups have finished explaining their recipes, they can be compiled into a cookbook by the students. Each person in class can assume a different responsibility in publishing it (e.g., editors, illustrators).

Contributor

Hilda Freimuth is ESL Coordinator at the Trilingual Language School, in Toronto, Canada.

Quiz Show

Levels
Beginning +

Aims
Glean, organize, and
describe relevant
information

Class Time
30–40 minutes

Resources
Varied collection of real
objects for prizes

Although it is sometimes taken for granted that organizational skills from the L1 will be transferred to the second or foreign language, this is not always so for many students. The aim of this activity is to encourage students to focus on information that will be pertinent to their particular writing task, allowing for easier organization and presentation of material.

Procedure

1. This is a writing game which has been successfully carried out with adolescents and adults.
2. Collect or purchase some objects that you can give away as prizes. These objects should be varied in design and texture so that students are exposed to a wide range of describing words and are also challenged to think of alternatives. The more unusual the object is, the more challenging it will be. If you have more than eight students in the class, you will need to think of a prizes that would be divisible: a small box of candy, a packet of nuts, multiple copies of a picture, flowers, pebbles, and so on.
3. If you have more than eight students in the class, divide the class into small groups, three to eight students in each group. You should preferably not have more than eight groups of students in the class.
4. Inform the students that you have a number of prizes to give away, but that to win any of the prizes, they will have to describe the object accurately. Because they do not know what each item is, they will have to get the information from you. To do so, they will need to write down a total of 10 questions that you will answer. However, to start, the students should only write down three questions. When they know the answers to those questions, they can then ask two more questions, and so on. Advise them not to waste their questions, but to consider what questions would enable them to get the neces-

sary information to be able to describe what the article looks like. Allow all types of questions.

5. Go round the class and answer the questions as each group or individual completes the first three questions. With large classes, encourage them to raise their hands when they have phrased the questions.

6. When each person or group finishes the first three questions, ask them to go on and write down two more questions, and so on, until they have used up their 10 questions.

7. They then have to describe the object and should write their descriptions on transparencies or on white paper that can be hung up around the class.

8. Reveal the object.

9. The class reads the descriptions of the other groups or individuals.

10. The class decides which description is the best. Act as an intermediary in case of dispute.

11. The class now looks at the questions which the winning group asked and compares the questions with their own.

12. Begin the game again with a second object. Again they start off with three questions, then two, and so on.

Caveats and Options

1. Although the ideal would be to have one question at a time, it will make it very difficult of you to answer the questions swiftly enough to keep up the pace. Some students may try to ask you what the object is. Be vague. For example, the object may be a plastic tumbler. A student or group may ask the teacher, "What is the object?" You can be vague and answer "Something you can find in a shop." That forces them to focus on getting a description rather than guessing what the object is.

2. Ten questions are recommended for intermediate and high intermediate students. More questions may be necessary for beginners.

Contributor

Hyacinth Gaudart is Associate Professor at the Faculty of Education, University of Malaysia.

Make a Poster

Levels
Beginning; children and
adolescents

Aims
Use known vocabulary
and structures to create
a paragraph

Class Time
30 minutes +

Preparation Time
3 minutes

Resources
Students' readers and
workbooks

It is important for students to have concrete evidence of their achievements. Posters, prominently displayed in the classroom, provide this.

Procedure

1. Have students choose an illustration in their reader or workbook that they would like to use in a poster.
2. Photocopy (and perhaps enlarge) that illustration.
3. Have students color the photocopy.
4. Have students write a paragraph explaining/describing/reacting to the illustration.
5. Ask students to discuss and refine the paragraph with you.
6. Have students mount their illustration and paragraph on a sheet of colored construction paper.
7. Ask students to sign, date, and display their work in the classroom (all year if possible so improvement can be noted).

Contributor

Victoria Marone has taught ESL to children and adults in the United States and Japan.

Action Logging

Levels
Beginning +

Aims
Communicate real
feedback to the teacher
Review class material
and expand upon class
notes for later study

Class Time
A few minutes

Resources
Handout (see
Appendix)

Real communication about real things motivates students to write. When they discover they can write about classroom events and influence your teaching, then their writing has a real purpose. You can become aware of individual needs and desires through the writing. Students and teachers are then purposefully interested in reading it to improve classroom teaching and the rapport with individual students that is often difficult in a group setting improves.

Procedure

1. Prepare a handout like the one in the Appendix.
2. In each class, you can ask them explicitly to write about things that you are specifically eager to get their reactions to.
3. Set a time for collecting or dropping logs off. I have different classes drop their logs off on different days of the week outside my office. (Optionally, you could also give them the last 5 minutes of class and collect them in class.)
4. Read the notebooks, writing comments where appropriate.
5. Return the logs in the next class or have students pick them up at a designated time.

Caveats and Options

1. Note that these are not normal diaries in that students write only about things related to class. I've been pleasantly surprised for several years with the gold mine that I have discovered in their logs.
2. Note also that this is not a dialogue journal and teacher responses are usually short, except when individuals show a special need. I've done it with more than 150 students a week for 2 years. It usually takes me about a minute a log to read and comment. Ninety percent of the

comments are short phrases like *Thanks for the feedback, you're doing great!* with perhaps a smiling face and my initials. Obviously responses are longer at the beginning of the term to let students know I appreciate their help. I tag certain pages for photocopying for my research projects and make photocopies of them to keep in my files.

Appendix: Action Log Requirements

After every class, as soon as possible (so you remember well what happens), write a short description of the class. Say briefly what we did and comment about what you learned and what you liked. List the different activities and segments. You may want to take short notes in class to remind you. Comment on those you especially liked and could learn from, and on those you didn't like and you think could be improved. I need your feedback so that I can teach you better. I read your Action Logs. I like your suggestions and will try to use them if possible.

Always put the date of the class and the time you write.

Always use people's names when you refer to partners.

A sample entry: April 8 (written April 8, 21:00)

1) DID: Today we listened to a story, did shadow-echoing, reformulation, speed reading and sang a song.
2) Comment: Shadow-echoing seems especially interesting. I'm going to try it in my other classes. I didn't understand some of the points in speed reading: what is chunking? Sometimes Mr. [Author] spoke too fast. Please speak slower. My partners were Yuki and Hiroko and it was fun to get to know them. We got a lot of homework, but it looks like fun. I'm looking forward to the rest of the classes. Oh, and I like singing.

If you have anything else that you think I should know (that influences your learning) please tell me (e.g., outside problems).

Contributor

Tim Murphey teaches in the Faculty of Foreign Languages, Nanzan University, in Nagoya, Japan.

Creating a Clear Picture

Levels
Beginning +

Aims
Write good, visual
descriptions

Class Time
2 hours

Resources
Heavy stock paper
sheets
Colored marker pens,
masking tape, notebook
paper
Several thesauruses

This activity helps students describe scenes vividly. The activity will lead into a descriptive essay.

Procedures

1. Walk around the classroom and put sheet of paper on the back of each student with masking tape. Each student selects a colored marking pen to use for the exercise.
2. Ask students to stand and walk around the room. They are to look at their classmates and then write some kind of description that describes the person on her back. They can refer to physical looks, personality, interest. All descriptions must be positive. They should not use hurtful or rude descriptions. Example: *lovely smile, beautiful, expressive, green eyes, generous and kind*.
3. Once involved in this activity, students get noisy and really enjoy it. Walk around and help students with spelling or mention whether or not the phrases they are using are descriptive enough.
4. You should also write on each student's back. Students especially like to read what the teacher has written.
5. When all students have a completed sheet on their backs, they may sit down and take the paper off and read what it says. It is enjoyable to watch their reactions as they read about how their classmates have described them.
6. Ask the students if the descriptions of them are accurate. Explain that these short descriptions are almost cryptic and that to write a good description clearly, we must use full, clear, descriptive sentences that visually show the person.
7. Have them think about a person they know well (mother, sister, brother, best friend) that they would like to describe. Have each

student write some long descriptive paragraphs about the person. They should cover the person's looks, character, personality and interests, so we can imagine what kind of person this is.

8. Have students break into small groups and share with members what they have written. Have them choose the most descriptive one. Have the person who wrote it read it to the class. Then have students discuss why it succeeds as a good description.

9. Have students revise what each has written by using a thesaurus to find other ways of saying things. Have several thesauruses available.

10. Have students help each other in revising as you walk around the room making suggestions.

Caveats and Options

1. I have used this method for several years and always found it to be successful. The students enjoy it because it involves physical activity and conversation. It also helps a shy student become involved. I recently had an introverted young man who didn't want to participate in this exercise. I told him that I would be the first to write on his back; he accepted this and soon got involved with the other students. I believe he was afraid of what students would write about him because he didn't have many friends, but realized that if I started off the list on his back, it would be positive and okay. Most students find it odd when you start putting the paper on their backs but soon realize there is nothing to worry about.

2. This activity leads into more in-depth essays using description and works with all ability levels.

Contributor

Anita Storck is an instructor at Chapman University, Orange, California, in the United States.

Describing Countries

Levels
Advanced

Aims
Describe own or
another country

Class Time
40 minutes

Resources
The map of the
country/countries you
want to deal with (see
Appendix for example)

Teaching writing includes so many activities starting with guided exercises, followed by preproductive and productive exercises. Describing people and things is the most popular, even in the L1. This activity asks students to focus on describing countries they have visited during holidays and business trips.

Procedure

1. Distribute the text among students who have been divided into pairs. You can use one big map for the whole class or have the map attached to every text.
2. Ask the students to read the text and fill in the gaps.
3. The students ask each other questions (you can be included as well) in order to check their work.
4. In 1 minute they can write the names of famous or remarkable natural features in Africa.
5. The students exchange their information by question-answer technique and trying to find the places in the map.
6. Then they can write a short passage about the country in order to summarize the facts.
7. At home, the students will write about their own country or its part:
   - climate and the character of the country
   - natural resources
   - population
   - industry
   - towns and villages.

Appendix: Map of Africa, With Passage

Using the attached map of Africa, fill in the following passage:

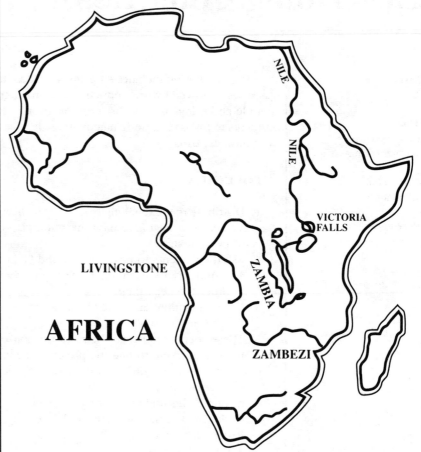

Africa has many places of interest. You can travel for days by train or by car and the country around hardly changes. And suddenly you come to a scene which makes you forget the dull journey before. This is certainly the case when you approach V_____ F_____ in Zambia, central _____ . The _____ are within easy reach of L_____, a little town in the south-west corner of _____ the town is named after Dr. Livingstone, the famous _____ . The main street turns south straight down a hill. As you look down it, you see a cloud rising in the distance. It is called "the smoke that thunders."

The six-mile drive takes you to the banks of the river _____ . At the seventh mile the river seems to end suddenly in a waterfall. There you are at the Eastern Cataract. The waterfall there is 300 feet deep and some hundred feet wide. At the _____ Cataract you may, if you wish, descend the steep steps with the help of a handrail. It will bring you near the foot of the _____ where you can look up at the mass of water shooting over the ledge above.

Contributor

Eva Tandlichova is Associate Professor and EFL teacher educator in the Department of English and American Studies at Comenius University in Bratislava, Slovakia.

Musical Comparison and Contrast

Levels
Low intermediate +

Aims
Describe similarities and
differences

Class Time
1 hour

Resources
Two short songs or
pieces of music that are
clearly different from
each other
Portable cassette
recorder
Diagram on the board
Collection of student-
generated descriptions
to write in the diagram
Student writing

This activity introduces comparison and contrast. Students can learn to organize descriptions of similarity and differences in a graphic way on the board and to use these bits of language to complete a paragraph comparing and contrasting the two pieces of music. Begin with music for low intermediate students. Comparing and contrasting written text may be more successful after students have a better idea of what they are looking for. By using music, you won't have to rely on text comprehension to generate the activity.

Procedure

1. Tell the students that they will listen to two pieces of music. Ask the students to describe what they hear using words or phrases. These directions can be written on the board as reinforcement for the lower level learners.
2. Play one piece of music at a time. I have found that students usually like to hear the pieces twice.
3. After listening to the first piece, wait 1 or 2 minutes until students have completed taking their last notes.
4. Repeat the process with the second piece of music.
5. Draw two large intersecting circles on the board. Label the circles, for example, Song 1 and Song 2. Pass around pieces of chalk and invite the students to write their descriptive notes on the board in the appropriate circle. Tell the students that this exercise will help them to see how the songs were different.
6. Draw students' attention to the space where the two circles intersect. Prompt students with questions about what this space might be for. Discuss the intersecting space as a place to write notes about how the songs were the same.

7. When the students have finished generating language on the board, discuss what they have written. This is a good opportunity to do some vocabulary instruction and to elicit further information where meaning is unclear.
8. Introduce the terms *comparison* and *contrast*. Write these terms on the board.
9. These students should be familiar with paragraph writing. Ask them to write a paragraph using the notes on the board about how the two songs were the same, and about how they were different.
10. After students have written their paragraphs, they may ask to reread their writing while listening to the tow pieces again. Offer this possibility.
11. A good follow-up activity would be to type up some of the student paragraphs to use as transparencies. Use these as a way to introduce comparison connectors and cohesive devices. Show students appropriate places to work these connectors into the text.
12. Have students share their writing.

Contributor

Josephine A. Taylor teaches in the Department of Applied Linguistics and ESL at Georgia State University in the United States.

Part IV: Personal and Business Correspondence

Editor's Notes

Writing probably evolved in association with trading. Some of the earliest written documents deal with the minutiae of goods and consignments, facilitating the transaction of business over time and space. Even in today's electronic world, business correspondence remains a highly significant writing function, as does the writing of notes, letters, and postcards, all of which serve the function of maintaining interpersonal as well as mercantile relationships.

The classroom provides a useful forum for both personal and business writing. The classroom exchanging of notes, so often a subversive activity, can be put to good use, while writing business letters to actual correspondents for a real purpose can provide a motivating element of task authenticity.

Correspondence also provides a useful context for developing the concepts of register and style: What we write casually to friends will be different from what we write to an unknown business correspondent. Features of format, organization and content, together with the ritualized forms of greeting and close, are also important aspects of both personal and business correspondence, all of which have to be learned and practiced.

This section will offer some useful variations on familiar writing types and tasks as well as new and imaginative ways of exploiting them.

◆ Personal Correspondence
Vacation Mystery Letter

This activity asks students to use English during vacation time when many lose momentum with their study, encourages them to interact with a student that they may not know well and thus improve the affective environment of the class, gives them the chance to practice writing a personal letter, stimulates curiosity about who has written the letter, and thereby gives students a good reason to look forward to the first day back in class after a vacation.

Procedure

1. This activity assumes that your students already have experience writing personal letters, but you should review the basic structure by either providing them with a sample or writing a short letter on the board or OHP. Besides language typically used in greetings and closings, you should point out that we often write about what we have done recently and what we plan to do.
2. Have students write their names and addresses on a sheet of paper. Cut this into strips and let students pick a piece of paper, making sure that no student has his own name and address.
3. The students' task will be to write a letter to the person whose name they have chosen. As described above the letter should contain some basic information about what the student has done so far in the vacation and what they plan to do. The student should not sign the letter.
4. During the first class after vacation, there are two possible procedures. The simplest is for students to tell the class who they think wrote the letter and why. If the classes are large or you think that students may have difficulty guessing who wrote the letter, they can stand up, circulate, and find the student who wrote them the letter by asking

about the information in the letter. For example: "Did you go to the movies on New Years Day?" or "Did you visit relatives in Osaka?"

5. You can conclude here or consider this a first draft and have students work with the person who received their letter to rewrite it. This draft can then be turned in to you.

Contributor

Eric Bray is Academic Director at the Kyoto YMCA English School, Kyoto, Japan.

Letter to the Editor

Levels
Advanced

Aims
Persuade, argue,
complain

Class Time
1 hour

Resources
Several different, recent,
local newspapers
Sample letter to the
editor

This activity challenges advanced students to use their skills of persuasion and argumentation. It requires a lot of thinking and experimentation in writing on the part of the learners with an added benefit: the chance that their letters will be published and possibly others will respond.

Procedures

1. Ask students what a letter to the editor is and what it is used for.
2. Discuss possible ideas for letters to the editor. Have students look at samples of letters to the editor. How are they written? What are the writers trying to do?
3. Organize students into small groups or three or four and give each a current local newspaper. Ask the students to take some time, 10–15 minutes, and look over the newspaper for interesting articles, problems, or anything else (e.g., too many ads) in order to generate ideas for letters to the editor.
4. As homework, give the students a couple of days to come up with an idea and to draft a letter to the editor. On the day you collect the drafts, ask everyone to bring a stamped envelope to the next class. (This gives them enough time to get a stamped envelope while you read what they have written).
5. In the next class, make quick revisions with the students and ask them to rewrite the letter one more time as homework. Tell students the letters will be mailed at the beginning of the next class.
6. Mail the letters and watch the newspapers.

Caveats and Options

It is likely that once the letters are mailed, the students will eagerly watch the newspaper to see if their letters appear. When the letters do appear, often the students will read each other's letters as well as rebuttals—which offers good reading practice.

Contributor

Shawn Clankie is currently in the graduate program in linguistics at the University of Cambridge, in the United Kingdom.

Send That Postcard

Levels
Intermediate +

Aims
Request information

Class Time
20–30 minutes

Resources
One blank stamped
postcard/student
One handout of the
addresses of state tourist
boards/student
(obtainable from most
almanacs)
One handout of the
format/student
Chalkboard or overhead
projector (OHP)

This activity gives students a practical reason for writing for which they will receive some benefit. Students tend to remember the format because of the information they receive by mail later. Once they have learned the format, the other possible uses are many (e.g., requesting college information).

Procedure

1. About 15 minutes before the end of a prior class, introduce the exercise. Begin by asking what states the students have visited and what they did and saw. Then ask them which states seem interesting to them. Announce that students will have the opportunity to write to a state to request tourist information. Tell students that they must pick one state to request information from and to bring one blank stamped postcard to the next class.
2. During the next class, go around the room asking which states were selected. Ask some students why they selected that state.
3. Demonstrate the format by first drawing two large rectangles on the blackboard or OHP. In the rectangles, create the sample postcards on the following page.

Dear Illinois Board of Tourism,

  I would like to learn more about your state. Could you please send me some tourist information? Thank you.

Signature
Student Name
Address

Return address

Stamp

Illinois Board of Tourism
Address

Header

Reason for writing
Request for information in conditional

Expression of gratitude

Name and address for information to be mailed to

Return address

Stamp

Mailing address

4. Hand out the list of addresses to each student along with a copy of the format and allow the students about 10 minutes to fill in their postcards. Walk around and make sure all students have correctly filled in cards.
5. Collect postcards and mail after class.

Caveats and Options

1. This may be used as a sole exercise or as a prewriting exercise for a longer essay based on the information the student receives. The abundance of brochures, maps, and guides these offices send out offer innumerable opportunities for later classes, not only in writing but also in discussion and reading.
2. Used as a prewriting exercise, during the down time while requests are in the mail, students can begin brainstorming ideas about the states they've selected. Once the information is received, the students may be given a follow-up essay topic as an introduction to what the state has to offer. If each student has a different state, after the essays are completed, they may orally introduce their state to the class in the form of a presentation.

This activity can lead to many others.

Contributor

Shawn Clankie is currently in the graduate program in linguistics at the University of Cambridge, in the United Kingdom.

In My Opinion

Levels
Advanced

Aims
Express an opinion in writing

Class Time
45–50 minutes

Resources
Magazine article on a controversial issue
Excerpts from readers letters expressing opinions about the article and the issue (see Appendix)

This activity integrates all skills and gives students opportunity to deal with authentic language in a real-life task. By discussing the pros and cons about an article, students move, in a paced fashion, through the process experienced by readers to build up a body of opinions from a text. The letter excerpts provide samples to guide the students as they attempt to learn ways of writing their arguments in a less informal style. The topic motivates the students to carry out the tasks throughout the activity and should be carefully selected among the range of current articles and letter excerpts available, always bearing in mind the students' interests, age, and experience.

Procedure

1. Divide the class in pairs or small groups and give each group one or two different letter excerpts to read and discuss. Ask the students to infer from the information in the excerpts the content, arguments, and information that may have motivated readers to write the letters.
2. As each pair or group presents their suggestions to the class, write their ideas on the board.
3. Give out copies of the main article and ask students to check whether their suggestions match the content of the text. Discuss any discrepancies and possible reasons that led students have different expectations about the article.
4. At this stage, encourage students to discuss the issues raised by the main article—this can be done again in pairs or small groups—and ask them to note their own arguments and ideas about the issues, for example, whether they agree or not with the arguments in the main article and why. A variation to the straightforward group discussion could be a role-play activity or simulation involving characters mentioned in the article.

233

5. After the ideas have been discussed, go through the letter excerpts with the whole class and elicit samples of language which can be considered typical in such type of text, for example, giving opinion, and differences in register/style between expressing opinion orally and in written form (refer to the speaking activity just carried out in Step 4).

6. Once students have been exposed to the language samples and have a list of their own opinions, ask them to write the main paragraphs (or the whole text) of a letter they would like to send to the magazine, expressing their views on the article they have read. The actual writing can either be done in class or as homework.

7. A follow-up activity may be to ask students to show their letters to the rest of the class on a wall display and elicit comments about both the content and the language in them.

Appendix: Sample Handout

Sample excerpts from letters on the topic legalization of marijuana:

. . . I was moved by the photos about drug-addicted adolescents in countries where neither the laws nor the society have been able to prevent the young from stepping into hard drugs [September 25]. As a mother I keep asking myself whether my two teenager boys should have a legal opportunity to experiment with joints, perhaps under parental supervision? This would make it less of a burden for families, schools and the police force! Dorothy Grass, *Wonderland*

. . . After reading about the arguments in favor of legal drug use in this country [September 25, Legalization of Marijuana] I wonder: is it acceptable that reliable professionals such as doctors encourage a habit which will certainly rot the minds and lives of our population? Jeff Shocked, *Fin-du-Monde*

(Students' names are pseudonyms)

Contributor

Douglas Altamiro Consolo teaches at the State University of Campinas, Brazil.

Writing Messages and Notes

Levels
Low intermediate +

Aims
Practice a writing activity applicable to daily life

Class Time
1 hour

Resources
Chalkboard or overhead projector (OHP)
Message cues handout (see Appendix)

This activity introduces the writing of letter and job applications.

Procedure

1. Use the chalkboard or OHP to illustrate an example of formal and informal messages generated by you, the students present, or previous students. Have students pick out elements of the messages that identify them as formal or informal, for example, slang, casual greetings, polite formulas.
2. After a discussion of when and how to use each writing style, pass out the handout on which are written cues for students to generate their own messages. Encourage students to add individual details to their messages to match their own experiences.
3. After writing several messages covering a variety of topics and styles, have students model their messages on the chalkboard and encourage comment from the other students in terms of appropriateness of style, expression, and grammar.

Appendix: Sample Message Cues Handout

1. You have arranged to meet your roommate at a restaurant at 8 p.m. tonight, but you realize that you have to spend the evening in the library to study for a test tomorrow. Write a note to your roommate telling her that your plans have changed.
2. On Monday, you missed your economics class. You go to see your professor to give him an explanation, but he is not there. Write a note giving your explanation of why you were not in class.
3. You have some important information to give to your friend, but when you go to his apartment, he isn't home. Leave a note telling him the information.

4. You have a problem in your apartment and you go to see the landlord, who unfortunately, is not at home. Write a note explaining your problem and requesting her assistance as soon as possible.

5. You girlfriend is coming over to your apartment at 6 p.m., but you won't be able to get there until 6:30 p.m. Write a note to leave on your door telling your friend to wait or where to meet you later.

6. Your daughter was sick last week and had to stay home from school. Write a note to her teacher explaining her absence.

7. Your mother is going shopping later today, but you forgot to ask her to get some food items for your camping trip this weekend. Write your mother a note asking her to pick up some food for you.

8. You want to play tennis after work today, but you forgot to ask your partner. Leave a message asking him to call you at work to arrange a time.

9. Your friend lent you a book that you needed to complete an assignment. When you return the book he is not home. Write a note thanking him for the loan of the book.

10. Think of a situation recently in which you had to leave a note for someone. Write down what you said in your note.

Contributor

Helen S. Huntley lives and works in New Freeport, Pennsylvania.

Advertisement Writing

Levels
Advanced

Aims
Discuss, read, revise, and edit an advertisement

Class Time
2 hours

Resources
Newspapers

This activity makes students aware that writing is a creative process that involves writing, prewriting, drafting, and rewriting. Throughout these different stages, students explore topics, develop ideas, and self-assess their work together and with you.

Procedure

1. Give students the following writing task:

> You are the advertiser of an advertising company. You received a memo from the property agent who would like you to prepare an advertisement for Mr. Chan, who wants to make a quick sale of his house. There is a rumor that this is a haunted house because 10 years ago, a woman was murdered here. Below is some more information about the house. Read through it carefully before starting to draft the advertisement.
>
> - A house with three bedrooms, one study, one sitting room and one dining room, master bedroom with sea view, garage, garden
> - fully furnished, carpeted, quiet, roomy
> - close to the bus stops, big supermarket, 10 minutes' drive by car to subway or town center
> - Marina Club with a wide range of recreational facilities nearby.

2. Hold an open, brainstorming session, asking students to answer the following:

- Do you have you any advertisements that you find impressive? If you do, describe it briefly to your classmates.
- Personally, do you believe what the advertisements tell you?

3. Ask students to do some individual writing in class following this procedure:

- Skim through two advertisements.
- Write one sentence to summarize the main idea of each advertisement.
- Write a paragraph to say which advertisement you like more and give reasons. You have 5 minutes to write on this. Just keep on writing. Write whatever comes to mind. Don't worry about the organization and the mistakes.

4. Ask students to read one anothers' work.

- Exchange your paragraph with your partner. Read his silently. Focus only on meaning. Put a *?* by any part you don't understand.
- Give your comments at the bottom to say whether you agree or disagree with your partner's viewpoint.
- Return the paragraph to your neighbor and ask him to clarify the parts you have questioned.
- Then give each other suggestions on how to elaborate the ideas better.

5. Help students identify their readers and purposes.

- Spend 3 minutes thinking about the format, structure and style of an advertisement. The following questions might help you.

    a. Who are going to be your readers? What is your relationship with the readers? For these readers, should your style be formal, neutral or informal? Should your tone be personal or impersonal?
    b. How much shared background information have you and your readers got on the product you are going to sell? How will this

decide the structure of your writing and the kind of information to be included?

c. What is your purpose in writing? In order to achieve your purpose, what sort of language device are you going to use, for example, emotive, persuasive, concrete, or abstract words?

d. How is a persuasive essay writing different from an advertisement in terms of presentation?

- In a group of three or four, discuss the above.
- Afterward, hold an open discussion with the teacher.

6. Have students decide how to present their advertisement.

- Decide on the presentation for your advertisement with your group members and give it a headline.
- Work together with your group on advertisement's structure in the following ways:

a. Discuss with your group members the possible areas of content in your advertisement and the points you would like to put under them.

b. Arrange the points in logical order and produce a rough plan in note form.

c. Report the plan and the way of presentation you have chosen to the rest of the class. Get suggestions from the teacher and classmates, and make comparisons between yours and theirs so as to improve it.

d. Revise your plan with your group members.

7. Ask students to draft the advertisement, using a loop writing technique:

- Based on the improved plan, start to write your introduction. It should not be long. A few sentences are enough.
- Focus on how to make your ideas interesting; otherwise you cannot draw your readers' attention to read your advertisement. It doesn't matter if you make grammatical mistakes.

- Write the main body of your advertisement. Expand your notes and put in new ideas if they come to mind. Make changes as you write because your plan is just a guide.
- Pay attention to the use of vocabulary. You need to use abstract and exaggerated language when describing the features of the house, but at the same time concrete information is also necessary.
- Write your conclusion. You have to be persuasive but avoid giving your readers a feeling that you are too forceful.
- Exchange your draft with your partner. Read your partner's silently. At this stage, just read for meaning. Put a *?* when you don't understand what she means. Give the point a written mark if you find the idea is good.
- Discuss the problems in the writing and possible improvements.
- Revise the content of your draft. Rewrite unclear ideas. Elaborate ideas whenever necessary.

8. Ask students to evaluate one another's work:

- With the teacher, discuss an evaluation checklist and a sample of your work.
- Exchange your revised draft with your partner. Read your partner's draft, and this time concentrate on the logical organization and the development of ideas, for example, how you linked ideas with conjunctions and transitional sentences.
- Return the draft to your partner. Discuss ways to improve the organization. I will join in your discussion.
- Revise the draft.
- Submit the draft to me.

9. Have students revise and edit their work:

- With your partner, discuss ways to improve your draft based on my comments and marking. At this item, you have to focus not only on organization and flow of ideas, but also on grammatical accuracy.
- Start to do the editing and if you have anything you are not sure of, ask me and group members for help.

- Exchange your final draft with your partner. Proofread your partner's and give comments.
- Make final changes before submission.

Caveats and Options

1. This activity can also be adapted to personal letter writing. Give the students a situation like the following as the assignment.

   Your pen friend is about 17 years old, and recently she has met a boy she likes very much, and have started going out quite often. However, when her parents discover this, they are very upset and stop her from seeing him. As a result, her relationship with her parents is getting very tense. She is extremely depressed about this, and she does not know what to do. Recently she has written to you and asked for your advice. In the letter she told you she had thought of leaving home or even committing suicide. Write your reply letter.

2. Brainstorming questions for this letter situation include, *What do you think about puppy love? Have you or any of your friends ever experienced puppy love? Do you like writing letters? Have you ever written to your friend to give advice to her about this problem?*

3. Have students read and summarize letters from the letters to the editor column in the newspaper as a warm up exercise.

Contributor

Winnie Lee teaches at the English Language Study Centre, in Hong Kong.

Dear Editor

Levels
Intermediate +

Aims
Practice writing
arguments

Class Time
40 minutes

Resources
Controversial letter to
the editor of an English
language newspaper,
with a few subsequently
published responses

Using current, controversial issues such as those we find in letters to the editor columns as stimulus, this activity motivates students to communicate their own ideas in response to a real letter to the editor. The activity also enables students to practice creative writing to support a point of view.

Procedure

1. Briefly explain the activity to the students: Students will read a letter to the editor and write a response.
2. Give a student a copy of a relatively short, recent and controversial letter to the editor and ask them to read it silently.
3. Divide students into groups of three or four and ask them to discuss whether they agree or disagree with the writer of the letter.
4. Rearrange the groups, maintaining the same group size. Those who agree with the letter will come together and discuss why they agree, and those who disagree with the letter will discuss why they disagree. Each group should appoint a secretary to jot down the main points of the discussion.
5. Ask the group to write a letter of their own, stating why they agree or disagree with the writer of the letter. They should plan carefully what ideas to include in the letter and suggest how those ideas are to be organized.
6. Tell students to write a first draft of this letter individually.
7. Allow students to form pairs and peer correct each other's letters.
8. Tell students to revise and write the final draft individually as homework.

9. Show the students some real responses and let them discuss in groups or pairs whether the real responses are better written and why (or why not).

Caveats and Options

1. For weaker students, consider designing a worksheet for preteaching purposes, for example, of vocabulary.
2. As a follow up, prepare transparencies to illustrate useful expressions needed for particular language functions, for example, how to express agreement or disagreement politely or polemically.
3. Vary the topic and approach to create and maintain interest. Probably best every 3 or 4 weeks.
4. Vary Steps 6 and 7 as follows: Divide the class into two groups and ask one group to write a letter agreeing and the other group disagreeing with the writer. Pair up the students with opposing views to discuss or debate the issue.

Contributor

David C. S. Li teaches in the English Department of the City University of Hong Kong.

Letters of Complaint

Levels
Intermediate

Aims
Learn to complain in
writing

Class Time
40 minutes

Resources
Chalkboard or overhead
projector (OHP)

This activity sensitizes students to the differences in register between written and spoken forms. It comprises a series of lessons focusing on different language functions, for example, apologizing, giving invitations, offering congratulations, and offering condolences.

Procedure

1. Ask students if they have ever written a letter of complaint. Elicit from students what kind of things people complain about in writing, for example, faults in new consumer products, poor services, incorrect bills. Write these up on the board.
2. Using some of the examples on the board, establish who the students would write to if they were to write a letter of complaint. For example, about a faulty CD player, they would write to the shop manager.
3. In pairs ask students to simulate (a) a conversation with a friend about a CD player they have just bought, but which doesn't work properly, and (b) a phone call between a consumer with a complaint and the official person they are complaining to, for example, someone who has just bought a CD player that doesn't work properly and the manager of the shop they bought it from.
4. Ask students to write a letter of complaint to the manager of the shop.
5. In pairs ask students to discuss the differences between complaining

   - orally to a friend
   - orally to an official person, and
   - in writing to an official person.

6. Elicit differences from students and write them on the board in three columns: oral/friend, oral/official, written/official. The differences should include actual examples of language used.

7. Highlight the differences that have emerged among the three columns and focus on forms that would be appropriate for the letter. Then ask students to write another letter of complaint.

Contributor

Dino Mahoney teaches in the Department of English, City University of Hong Kong.

Writing in Character

Levels
Intermediate +

Aims
Describe events in the past
Explore personal reactions to those events
Give advice

Class Time
40 minutes

Resources
Appropriate literary texts

This activity asks students to explore a literary text by writing in the persona of tone of the characters in the text and in the persona of a friend of that character.

Procedure

1. Choose a central character in a book or play that the students may be reading, for example, Davey, in Judy Blume's *Tiger Eyes*.
2. Ask the students to imagine that they are that character, and that they are going to write a letter to a very good friend describing and analyzing how they feel about a certain event or person or situation, for example, Davey writing a letter to a friend expressing how she feels about her father's death and her move from Atlantic City to New Mexico.
3. Have students swap letters and reply to each other in the persona of the friend, giving advice.

References and Further Reading

Blume, J. (1982). *Tiger eyes.* New York: Macmillan.

Contributor

Dino Mahoney teaches in the Department of English, City University of Hong Kong.

Real-Life Writing

Levels
Intermediate +

Aims
Write letters and essay
in a real context
Learn research skills

Class Time
Varies

Resources
Address of an
international
organization

Students enjoy writing real letters to real people. They also like to collect their own course material. Here is a way of bringing these two enjoyable activities together, while also polishing students' letter- and essay-writing skills and introducing them to research skills.

Procedure

1. Find an international organization that sends free information to interested people. Pro environment groups, such as Greenpeace International, are ideal.
2. Before the semester begins, write a letter to the organization, asking if it is possible for them to send, for educational purposes, information packages to all the students in your class. You may also wish to specify the type of material you prefer: brochure, booklet, poster, for example.
3. At the beginning of the semester, have your students write a letter in class, asking for information on the organization's activities. Have pairs evaluate/correct each other's letters. Ask them to mail the letter. If the mail procedure goes well, your students should receive their information files in 3 or 4 weeks time.
4. During these weeks, have your students choose a topic that will be included in the information pack from the organization (e.g., air pollution, solutions for environmental pollution, rare or almost extinct animals), preferably something that requires research out of as well as in the library. Ask them to do research on this topic as concerns your surroundings (e.g., air pollution in your country); in addition to reading in the library, they may interview people, prepare a simple questionnaire and conduct a simple survey, or gather statistical data from local authorities.

5. In class, work on different essay types they could choose, such as narrative, descriptive, and comparison. Also, teach basic principles of quoting a source.

6. Have students write a rough draft of their essay using the data they have gathered so far. Have pairs evaluate each other's work.

7. When the material packs arrive, spend some time in class to make sure they are digested well.

8. Have students incorporate information from this material into their own essay.

9. Evaluate a student's work by these criteria:

- appropriateness of type and amount of information included
- ability to incorporate library or printed material with own research.

Caveats and Options

When the report/essays are finished, have student send them to the organization. Students especially enjoy the idea that they have produced something that is of value for an organization abroad.

Contributor

Selda Mansour, previously English for Academic Purposes Instructor at Eastern Mediterranean University in North Cyprus, is at present raising a trilingual child in Jordan.

Psst, Pass It On

Levels
Beginning +

Aims
Begin a writing class in
a nonthreatening way

Class Time
20–30 minutes

Resources
None

Many students come to writing class thinking that they cannot write well and stating that they do not like to write. This activity could set the tone for a writing class where all writing has value, all participants have the ability to write, the teacher is not the focal point, and writing can be enjoyable.

Procedure

1. Ask the students for a show of hands of how many like to write in their L1. Then ask how many like to write in English. The response will probably be disappointing.
2. Ask the students to imagine that they are back in elementary school, perhaps fifth grade. You may want to ask specific questions such as the name of the school or teacher, where they sat in the room, if they had to wear a uniform. Then ask if they were good students. Some, if not all, will admit to having been naughty at times. Encourage examples and add a few of your own. If nobody has mentioned passing notes to friends, suggest it. Ask who they wrote to and what the teacher did if he found a note. Beginning classes may need a good deal of mime and examples during this discussion.
3. Tell the students that they will now have a chance to write notes to their classmates, and they will not get in trouble for it. You will not even read their messages. Students can write questions or comments to anyone in the room. The only rules are:

   - write as many notes as possible
   - write only in English
   - sign and deliver your notes
   - don't talk at all.

249

Use torn pieces of notebook paper to set the informal tone. You might begin by tearing off a piece a paper and writing sample note and delivering it.

Once it is clear that everyone understands, begin timing. A minimum of 20 minutes is ideal for intermediate level students. If students later try to ask questions, motion that they must be silent and write the question. Although the silence is difficult for some people, it also makes the exercise much more exciting.

4. It is crucial that you participate as a writer. Some students may not be getting notes, and you will need to make sure that they do. This is also an excellent opportunity to communicate with students who are new to the program or school.
5. Students usually find it hard to stop writing at the end of 20 minutes.

Caveats and Options

1. A follow-up discussion is important. Most students will say that they enjoyed the exercise and that they didn't realize that they had been writing and reading for 20 minutes. This may be a good point to present the syllabus or course plan. While discussing the kinds of writing students will be doing, you may point out the direct relationship of this exercise to writing notes to co-workers or teachers, writing feedback during peer editing or the concept of writing for an audience, whatever is relevant to the particular class.
2. This exercise can be used midterm, at the end of the term or whenever the teacher senses the class could benefit from the opportunity to communicate freely.

Contributor

Marilynn Spaventa teaches in the ESL Department, Santa Barbara City College, in the United States.

Letter to an Art Gallery

Levels
Beginning +

Aims
Describe and persuade

Class Time
50 minutes

Resources
Pictures of art work
from gloss art
magazines

In this activity, students discuss the appropriate language for writing complaints and persuasive letters in English. Although the subject of this exercise is art, and the situation is purely imaginary, students can use these skills to communicate their needs effectively in many functions of their daily life.

Procedure

1. Introduce the topic of letter writing. Go over format requirements for a business letter and talk about appropriate language (modals, polite forms) and register.
2. Dividing the class into groups of four or five students, give each group a set of pictures of art objects, telling them to select one that they like or find interesting.
3. After everyone has selected a picture, tell the students to imagine that they are the artist who created the piece in the picture. Explain to the class that artists need to be good salespersons to persuade people to exhibit their work. They need to write a letter to the curator of an art gallery to describe their art work and persuade him to invite them to exhibit work at the gallery. (Give a fictional name and address to the curator and gallery, such as: Mr. Gerald Highpockets, New Wave Gallery, 24350 Palermo Blvd. Huntington Beach, CA 90032).
4. Have students peer edit the letters, allowing students to react to each other's writing and to offer advice and correction before revising their letters (at home) to be turned in the next class period.
5. Portions of the student writing, changed enough to protect identities, can be used for further class discussion about the relative effectiveness of some forms of language in U.S. culture.

Caveats and Options

The pictures should encompass several artistic styles. Care must be taken to avoid subjects that may be offensive to some students. There should be at least one picture per student.

Contributor

Beverly Walker-Watkins is Instructor of English and Fine Art in the Department of Humanities, Allegany Community College, in the United States.

◆ Business Writing

Creative Writing Tasks for the Workplace

Levels
Intermediate +

Aim
Practice writing
persuasive reports,
formal requests
Give information

Class Time
1 hour/task

Resources
Role cards
Possible answers

Procedure

Small-Group Task

1. Tell participants that they must imagine they are all working for the same company (this may be the case anyway). Their boss has told them that he intends to commission a follow-up course. He wants a schedule that suits their needs, so he has asked them to decide on a schedule for the next course. Remind them of the current arrangement, that is, 10 weeks, 3 hours a week, on Friday afternoons. Divide the class into small groups to discuss other ways of scheduling the course. They should come up with three or four alternative proposals.

2. At this point ask them how they are going to present the information to their boss. They may suggest just telling him orally in which case it's worth discussing why that may not be a good idea, that is, too much information to digest at one time, too many facts to remember. They may, of course, suggest a written report straight away.

3. Ask them to write the list of suggested alternatives and to write a summary of the arguments for and against each option. This will form the main body of the report.

4. At this point you can ask what else is necessary in the report. They will probably come up with the idea of introduction, conclusion, and recommendations but be unsure about what each section should contain and how each should be written. This can be discussed with each group.

5. The introduction would need to contain dates of the course, course title, perhaps names of participants, and number of hours to be spent training. The conclusion would normally make a decision and decide

which option is preferable and why. The recommendation would suggest future changes to the schedule and perhaps who should implement them.

6. The normal order of reports should then be discussed after which you should assign the report.

Large-Group Follow-Up

In the task just presented, the participants worked in small groups and presented the findings from a small group of people. This perhaps meant that individuals, preferences and restrictions may have been noted; names may even have been used.

This follow-up task involves drawing together the reports from the whole class and presenting the results drawn from a larger sample. This will contrast two styles of report writing: the narrow scope personal report with the wider ranging report that has to generalize. The participants will have to deal with large numbers of possible permutations and so will need to abstract and generalize.

1. Once groups have all completed a report representing their own group's ideas and findings, give each member of each group a different letter: A, B, C. and so on. Group the students so that all the As are together, likewise the Bs and Cs. This will ensure that the new groups contain at least one member from each of the previous groups.

2. The new groups then compare the information and findings of all the reports with the aim of writing a new report summarizing all the findings of the individual reports. The new report should be no longer than any of the previous ones. This will force the writers to summarize and generalize. Tables and other visuals are permissible. Stress that the report must reach a conclusion. One of the options must be agreed on.

3. Ask the report writers what the next step would normally be after the manager approves the report's recommendations. This should elicit the idea of checking with the institute concerned whether the new schedule is al right with them.

4. Discuss with the participants what the normal format for this communication would be. They may decide on a letter or a fax.

5. Discuss the relationship between the institute manager and the participants' organization. In other words, how formal does the letter need to be? What forms of address will they use? How will they sign off?
6. Then discuss what function the letter should perform. Is it a request? Does it tell the institute what to do? Is it a confirmation?
7. Finally, have them draft the letter.
8. The new schedule for the course has been agreed. Now all that remains is to notify the participants. What format will this notification have?
10. Draft the circular.

Contributor

Tim Gore is Manager of the Business Communication Unit of the British Council, in Hong Kong.

Business Letter as Storytelling

Levels
Intermediate +

Aims
Understand the format
of business letters
Write an acceptable and
effective letter

Class Time
30–40 minutes

Resources
Sample correspondence
(both sent and received)
requesting information
on a service or
complain about a
product or service
Overhead projector
(OHP) and
transparencies

To relieve the boredom of ordinary letter-writing lessons, introduce correspondence in a storytelling mode. Point out the important features of the letter-writing exercises as the story unfolds. More realistic letter writing is the usual result of this exercise.

Procedure

1. Save copies of your own letters of complaint and the subsequent interchange of correspondence with the respondent.
2. Make an OHP slide showing the format of the six main features of a business letter (heading, reference, salutation, body, closing, signature), perhaps with an overlay to show stylistic differences between hand-written and typed/word processed letters.
3. Hand the students photocopies of your initial letter with the six main features numbered to correspond with the OHP, as you are telling the first installment of the story behind the complaint. Point out the features in the photocopied letter.
4. Make an OHP slide showing the purpose of the paragraphs in the body of the letter (first paragraph establishing the history of the events, second paragraph stating the status at the moment and third paragraph outlining the expected action in the future) and the type of language used.
5. Continuing the story, hand a photocopy of the reply to your complaint and ask the students to identify the purpose of each paragraph. This can be done as pair work or as class discussion. (This step can precede Step 4 for more advanced classes, with Step 4 becoming a means of checking the understanding of the functions of the paragraphs.)
6. Ask the students to imagine a situation and write a letter of complaint/ request observing the correct format, paragraphing, and grammatical

structures. Guided letter-writing exercises can be devised for low intermediate learners.

7. As a variation to the writing phase, a word processor could be used and the letter in draft sent by e-mail to the teacher for comment, then to another student for a reply if a networked lab was available for use.
8. Letters can be redistributed in the class and replies to the complaints/requests written by other students as homework.
9. Monitor each student's understanding of the elements of the lesson by moving around the class during the writing stage.

Contributor

Norma Green is Senior Tutor and English for Academic Purposes Coordinator in the English Language Unit, at the University of Aberystwyth, Wales, in the United Kingdom.

Letters of Application

Levels
Intermediate

Aims
Convince the addressee
of the excellence and
suitability of the writer
for a specific position or
award

Class Time
50 minutes–1 hour

Resources
Handout of
requirements for each
application (see
Appendix)

This activity enables students to practice their letter-writing and persuasive skills in an activity similar to one they may be required to perform in real life.

Procedure

1. Have students brainstorm in class the kind of information they would need to include (or omit) in a letter of application and the appropriate language and style to use.
2. Hand out the cue sheet (see Appendix) and explain that the students should first make notes of items to include, basing their response on the facts of their own lives, but adding extra details to fit the requirements of each letter.
3. Have students write their first draft, then reread and consider the following question:

   - Are all the details relevant to the situation?
   - Do all the details contribute to making the writer appear in a positive light?
   - Are abstract statements backed up by concrete details?
   - Do you stand out as someone special and interesting?

4. Have students write their second drafts, paying attention to clarity and grammar.

Appendix: Application Cues

1. Every year, the Rotary Club provides several scholarships to undergraduates to attend a foreign university. A scholarship committee will review applications from students who can show a record of scholastic achievement, community and volunteer activities, and an interest in

learning foreign languages and experiencing different cultures. Interested students should write a letter to the President of the Rotary Club, Mr. John Smith, describing themselves and explaining their reasons for wishing to study in a particular country.

2. Mr. Mark Jones is a divorced father of two children, a boy aged 9 and a girl aged 6. The children are going to spend the summer with their mother in Spain, but because he cannot accompany them, he wishes to find a student willing to take care of the children on the trip to and from Spain. In return, the student will receive a return air ticket, plus expenses for the trip. Interested students are requested to write Mr. Jones a letter, describing themselves, their travel experience, and language proficiency in Spanish.

3. An international organization concerned with saving the environment is organizing a trip to the Amazon region to research plant and animal life. A number of scholarships will be awarded to students from different countries who can show achievement and commitment to the field of ecology and environmental concerns, as well as a background in international studies and languages. Applicants are requested to write a letter to the director, Dr. Margaret Adams, outlining their major interest and concerns for the environment, and the reasons for their desire to participate in the Amazon research.

Contributor

Helen S. Huntley lives and works in New Freeport, Pennsylvania.

Writing Appropriately

Levels
Intermediate +

Aims
Use appropriate style in writing business letters to achieve the writing objectives

Class Time
1 hour

Resources
Copies of inappropriately or ineffectively written business letters produced by nonnative speakers of English

This activity gets students to think about the objectives of business communication and analyze authentic written business correspondence products to compare intended effects with actual ones. Authentic materials will give students a touch of reality and enhance their awareness of communication objectives in a business context. Adult students with work experience could be asked to produce real samples of ineffective communication from their place of work for analysis. After acquiring such text-revising skills, students can apply them to their own writing.

Procedure

1. Ask students to consider the criteria for or qualities of a good business letter. Discuss them in class.
2. Distribute copies of a sample of an appropriately written business letter to the students (see Appendix for samples).
3. Give students 3 minutes to read the letter.
4. Divide students into small groups and ask them to consider the following questions (which you may either put on an overhead transparency for projection or write on the white board):

   - Do you think it is an effective letter?
   - What did the writer intend to achieve?
   - How well have the writer's objectives been met? Compare your first reaction to the letter with the way you think the writer intended you to react.
   - Identify the grammatical, lexical and stylistic problems in the letter which may have obscured the intended message and made the letter ineffective.

5. Let each group report to the whole class the problems identified.

6. Ask the students to rewrite the letter in small groups.

7. This lesson can be followed up by asking different groups to put their revised versions of the letter on transparencies for the whole class to comment on, using the same critical skills. For adult students, they can also bring back what they consider to be good examples of effective communication for discussion in the following lessons.

Appendix: Sample of Poorly Written Letter

Directions

The following is a draft of a letter of good-will to be sent to the clients at the end of the year, written by a sales manager of a chemical firm.

There are many problems with the letter which may have rendered it ineffective. Identify the grammatical, lexical and stylistic problems of the letter.

Working in a group of three or four, rewrite the letter for the sales manager.

Continued

Dear Friends/Customers,

As approaches to the end of the year, we would like to take this opportunity to extend our gratefulness for your whole-year patronage and support towards our chemical products and services.

Throughout the year, if any delay in our products delivery, insufficient services rendered by our technical representatives, or any negligence that cause you operation troubles, have been associated with our administration, we hope that you can accept our tolerable pardoning.

At the meantime, we are trying to evaluate and rectify the defects that persist in our administration so that operative efficiency as well a business economy can be closely related to our client's necessities. We'll be obliged to further reinforce or technical support and chemical expertise for the sake of your urgency.

You are kindly requested to express you constructive criticisms and valuable suggestions towards our policy so that corrective and operative improvement will be solidly executed at the start of the coming new year.

Wish you another successful year with our prompt services and efficient products.

Sales Manager
Lido Chemical Co.

Contributor

Wanda Poon is Principal Lecturer in the Division of Humanities and Social Studies at the City University of Hong Kong.

Authentic Texts for Writing Memos

Levels
Intermediate +

Aims
Organize an effective
memorandum

Class Time
90 minutes +

Resources
Sample office
memoranda
An editing checklist (see
Appendix)

Intermediate–level students may have may have a good general command of writing skills but be unable to produce writing that reflects the conventions of professional communication. Using authentic materials increases students' interest and motivation in learning how to write and also exposes them to models of effective writing.

Procedure

1. Collect examples of effective office memoranda of the type you want your students to practice writing themselves. (About six examples are sufficient.) Collect poorly written or weakly organized ones as well for text-revising practice. In addition, find an example of a checklist for writing effective memorandum that you feel will be useful to your students (see Appendix).
2. Distribute copies of the memorandum to pairs or groups of students.
3. Ask students to examine and compare the memoranda and to answer questions such as the following:

   - Where can you find information about the sender and the receiver of the message?
   - What function does the subject heading serve?
   - How many paragraphs are there in the examples? Are the paragraphs long or short?
   - Reading only the first paragraph, can you tell the main subject of concern in each example?
   - Do the sentences vary in length and type?
   - Do the writers use different tenses in their writings?
   - Can you spot any grammatical or spelling errors?
   - Compare the examples, how do the writers end the memo?

4. As the students work through the memoranda and the questions, ask them to develop a checklist that they think captures the essence of an effective memorandum. The checklist should consider issues of content, grammar, clarity, conciseness and style. Give them examples of what might be included in each element of the checklist, for example, under content, they might put *Include only necessary information*; under grammar, they might put down *Check the subject-verb agreement*.
5. Allow students up to 45 minutes for this activity and then have groups present their information.
6. Now distribute copies of your own editing checklist or writing guide.
7. Review the checklist and compare what each element includes with the information students have produced.
8. Summarize the main points of writing an effective memorandum and prepare students for the writing task.
9. Distribute copies of poorly written memorandum for the groups to analyze, using the checklist to guide them. (See Caveats and Options.)
10. Each group should suggest how the memorandum can be improved.
11. After discussion, students should rewrite the weak examples on group or individual basis.

Caveats and Options

An alternative is to omit the writing practice of revising the weak examples. Instead, go straight to the drafting of a memorandum on group or individual basis.

Appendix: Sample Editing Checklist

Content

☐ Use informative and specific headings.
☐ Paragraph by idea.
☐ Retain first choice words.
☐ Eliminate unnecessary details.
☐ Proportion should match emphasis.
☐ Check accuracy and completeness of factual information.

Grammar

- [ ] Do not write fragments for sentences.
- [ ] Avoid run-on or fused sentences.
- [ ] Do not dangle verbals.
- [ ] Use parallel structure.
- [ ] Make pronouns agree with their antecedents.
- [ ] Make verbs agree with their subjects.
- [ ] Do not change tenses or words unnecessarily.
- [ ] Punctuate correctly.
- [ ] Choose appropriate words and phases.
- [ ] Spell correctly.

Clarity

- [ ] Prefer short sentences and simple words.
- [ ] Use concrete words and phases over vague general ones.
- [ ] Sequence ideas to indicate emphasis.
- [ ] Link properly to show relationship.
- [ ] Show clear transitions between ideas.
- [ ] Use clear references.
- [ ] Place modifiers correctly.

Conciseness

- [ ] Prefer active-voice verbs and action verbs.
- [ ] Be emphatic and to the point.
- [ ] Highlight the main verbs of sentences.
- [ ] Cut cliches, redundancies and little-word padding.
- [ ] Eliminate needless repetition.

Style

- [ ] Vary sentence patterns and length.
- [ ] Substitute stronger verbs for weak ones.
- [ ] Prefer a personal, conversational tone.
- [ ] Adjust the tone and formality to suit the purpose and audience.

References and Further Reading

Booher, D. (1988). *Send me a memo: A handbook of model memos.* Hong Kong: Book Marketing.

Contributor

Pauline Tam is University Assistant Lecturer at the City University of Hong Kong.

Practical Business Writing

Levels
Low intermediate +

Aims
Inform someone or
request information

Class Time
30 minutes-1 hour

Resources
Paper
Appropriate addresses
and references
Three standard business
letters

G iving students a formula or a template for business letters, you foster confidence and facility with the language in a realistic situation while teaching both the process and the product. Because business letters need to be friendly and conversational as well as clear and correct, when students use a formula to write out the business conversation, they can plan, outline, write, revise, seek help, and revise again.

Procedure

1. Present the following 10 principles to summarize the basics of business letter writing:

   - Write concisely, eliminating stock phrases that serve no purpose, and using reasonably short sentences. Avoid jargon in favor of common words and phrases.
   - Consider the reader's background and expected attitude toward the message, tailoring the words to the reader's situation and level of understanding.
   - Write positively, eliminating negative words from the message.
   - Strive for clarity, using familiar words and ensuring that grammar, punctuation, and spelling are correct.
   - Check that the information in the message is accurate.
   - Look for omissions and inconsistencies to ensure completeness.
   - Strive for concreteness with specific amounts and figures, rather than abstract concepts.
   - Use active, rather than passive, constructions to foster clarity as well as brevity.
   - Ensure fairness—avoid evidence of stereotyping and prejudice.
   - Finally, practice ethicality, ensuring that no impossible promises are made, no matter how much goodwill they might create.

267

2. Present a business letter format and the guidelines for one of these three basic business letters:

Inquiry Letter
- State your request clearly in the first sentence, using a question or a polite request.
- Give background information that the reader might need to know to respond appropriately to the request.
- List specific question or items in separate paragraphs, and enumerate the items.
- End with a goodwill statement indicating that a response would be appreciated, and include any deadlines or addresses.

Order Letter
- Begin with a direct statement of the request (e.g., *Would you please send the following items.*)
- List the items in columns with column headings of quantity, catalogue number, description (e.g., color, size), unit price, and total price.
- Total the order, including shipping charges if known.
- Include payment terms, shipping, and deadlines.

Request for Assistance
- Begin with a statement requesting the help.
- Add any details about the conditions of performance by the reader—dates, times, quantities . . . .
- Describe any details about the results of the assistance (i.e., how the writer will use the assistance once it is received, or why the writer needs the assistance).

3. Ask students to write a letter similar to those suggested below:

- Write to the department chair of a program you plan to enter and ask about specific admission requirements and assistantships.
- Write to the Chamber of Commerce of a city to which you plan to move and ask about local conditions—for example, housing, cost of living, climate.

- Write to a daily newspaper of a city to which you plan to move and request subscription information (e.g., costs, frequency).
- Find a catalogue of international foods or other items with which the student is familiar. Ask the student to find one or more items that he or she would like to have, and have the student write an order letter.
- Have the student find a product ad in a magazine and have her write a letter to order the item.
- Give students mail order catalogues and ask them to find an outfit for some occasion, determine the sizes, and order the items. (This may be a wonderful culture lesson as well as a communication lesson. Another useful exercise might be to give students a budget and ask students to furnish an apartment.)
- Write to a university and ask for their current undergraduate/graduate catalogue and application forms for admission.
- Write to the financial aid office of a university and ask for scholarship information and application forms.
- Write to the student housing office of a university and ask for on-campus or off-campus housing information and application forms.
- Write to the Chamber of Commerce of a city to which you plan to move an request a copy of the local telephone book (useful item for finding addresses of, e.g., utility companies).

5. Have students evaluate their own or a peer's paper using the guidelines for the type of letter and also the 10 principles.
6. Mail the letters if appropriate.

Contributor

Janet Winter is Associate Professor in the Department of Management at Central Missouri State University, in the United States.

Also available from TESOL

Books for a Small Planet:
An Multicultural/Intercultural Bibliography
for Young English Language Learners
Dorothy S. Brown

Common Threads of Practice:
Teaching English to Children Around the World
Katharine Davies Samway and Denise McKeon, Editors

Discourse and Performance
of International Teaching Assistants
Carolyn G. Madden and Cynthia L. Myers, Editors

Diversity as Resource:
Redefining Cultural Literacy
Denise E. Murray, Editor

New Ways in Teacher Education
Donald Freeman, with Steve Cornwell, Editors

New Ways in Teaching Grammar
Martha C. Pennington, Editor

New Ways in Teaching Listening
David Nunan and Lindsay Miller, Editors

New Ways in Teaching Reading
Richard R. Day, Editor

New Ways in Teaching Speaking
Kathleen M. Bailey and Lance Savage, Editors

New Ways in Teaching Vocabulary
Paul Nation, Editor

Pronunciation Pedagogy and Theory:
New Views, New Directions
Joan Morley, Editor

Video in Second Language Teaching:
Using, Selecting, and Producing Video for the Classroom
Susan Stempleski and Paul Arcario, Editors

For more information, contact

Teachers of English to Speakers of Other Languages, Inc.
1600 Cameron Street, Suite 300
Alexandria, Virginia 22314 USA
Tel 703-836-0774 • Fax 703-836-7864